THE WHITETAIL DEER GUIDE

The Whitetail Deer Guide

HOLT, RINEHART AND WINSTON

New York   Chicago   San Francisco

For Marg
whose patience has been unending

Contents

Preface

 Whitetail deer are sought everywhere. They are very prolific, adaptable, and great on the table. More hours are spent in search of whitetail deer than any other big-game animal. I would like to make these hours more enjoyable. Hunting whitetails should provide enjoyment and relaxation rather than heavy work and grumbling.

I firmly believe that if you intend to hunt an animal, you should know as much as you can about it. You should know the type of terrain it will frequent, the foods it will choose over others at certain times of the year, its breeding habits, the times of day or night that it is particularly active, how it reacts to humans, how it uses cover, its means of communication, and the way it reacts to various kinds of weather.

Once you have learned the basic nature of the species you want to hunt, you can then decide what kind of equipment you should have, such as weapons, clothing, calls, scents, camping equipment, etc. You can also decide whether to hunt primarily for meat or trophy animals. Some game is fun to hunt on a combination-type hunt along with other game.

I am a firm believer that game is delicious on the table, and I am appalled at the amount of meat wasted by the American hunting public. The idea of all game having a "wild" taste is positively ridiculous. Almost all bad or poor meat is the result of improper handling. We will cover this thoroughly later. I have served all varieties of game in my dining room to people of all ages and standards. Hardly any could ever tell me what they were eating. Judging by the quantities of meat eaten, I'm sure they didn't object to any "wild" taste, although I did have a fellow once tell me the meat was tender but it certainly tasted "wild" when in fact he was eating a normally fine cut of beef! I must say I too have eaten some pretty wild and tough beef.

Hunting is changing as rapidly as the times. Some methods that worked years ago just don't apply to the modern animal. It is the purpose of this book to acquaint you with the habits of game and the methods of hunting and caring for the meat which are best suited to the world of today.

To become a consistently successful hunter of whitetail bucks you must become fairly proficient at all the different ways of hunting: trail watching, still-hunting, horn rattling, scrape hunting, driving, and decoying or calling. Weather, time of the year, woods conditions, food, and so forth all enter into the picture. You must be able to select the best method.

I know of only one bass fisherman who isn't stocked to the eyebrows with lures guaranteed to take bass. Instead, he insists on fishing with a spoon and pork rind combination . . . period. I will concede that this is a good lure, and in the hands of an expert, which he is, it produces very well, but I have seen him come home empty-handed when the switchers were catching plenty of bass. His philosophy is, "If they aren't going to hit my spoon and meat, to hell with 'em!" This may be okay for a bass fisherman who has nine or twelve months of the year to fish, but it's not good enough for the deer hunter who may have as little as two days to fill the bill.

I get very upset and impatient when there's no venison hanging on the buck pole! There is a method designed to fit each situation. You ought to see me if two days of the gun season go by and there's no meat hangin'!

There are ways that produce deer when other methods don't. It doesn't take a lifetime of living in the woods to know the right ways. It takes an insatiable appetite for learning, big ears, and practice (mainly off season). Athletes don't practice during the game; they practice before and after. Too many deer hunters watch the "boob tube" when they could be out enjoying themselves with their families and practicing.

It always amazes me how a man will spend a lot of money for a fine rifle, more on clothing and miscellaneous gear, take a vacation, drive a few hundred miles, rent a cabin or motel, and then not have the slightest idea what to do when he starts to hunt.

I'm old enough to know that reading this book will not

transform a city-bred smog breather into an Indian-footed super-hitter of whitetail deer overnight. The purpose of this book is to help shorten the novice period in the hunter's life, and to provide those tiny little gems of knowledge that experienced hunters are constantly searching for.

THE WHITETAIL DEER GUIDE

I. *The Hunter*

The duck hunter must rise early, be dedicated to the care and use of such specialized equipment as decoys, duck skiffs, stationary and portable blinds, motors, calls, hip boots or waders, duck guns, and retrieving dogs of some type. He must have considerable knowledge of duck haunts, a built in feel of when the ducks will be flying, and last but very important, a completely understanding wife who'll put up with such nonsense and cook whatever ducks he may bring in.

The upland game bird shooter may have to travel many many miles to find his game. A good dog is in order here too. It must find and retrieve the birds. The hunters must be a good wingshot to bag his game. He too must have an understanding wife who will look at the single ruffed grouse and the diminutive woodcock, then look at the three school-age kids and say, "Boys, look what Dad brought home for dinner tomorrow night. Gosh, won't we have a feast."

The rabbit and squirrel shooter is somewhat different, inasmuch as he may have the opportunity to hunt closer to home. The game he bags is generally shot up and crawling with fleas. As good as the little woman is about such things, the game better be dressed and cleaned before it arrives in the house or it generally gets consigned to the garbage can.

Who hunts the elusive whitetail deer? Anybody, yes anybody, can be a deer hunter. We come from all walks of life, in all shapes, sizes, colors, weights, personalities, ages, and sexes. Once you get the real deer fever, you're hooked. Deer hunters will hunt with fevers of 103 degrees to keep them warm, or hobble to their stands with casts on their legs. I know men who can't sleep at all the night before opening day. Cracked ribs or ulcers become meaningless on that occasion. I know one fellow who was to enter the hospital on a Friday for traction because of an injured back. He told the doctor he couldn't go until Monday. When the doctor asked him why, he said he had to be out for the opening, no matter what. The doctor told him okay, he wouldn't see him till Monday anyway because *he* had a date with a deer! Some businesses lock their doors for the season, and even schools don't chastise their wayward students.

Why do so many hunt the whitetail? Mainly because the animal is found in large numbers close to large population centers. Compared to hunting other big game, monetary outlays are minimal. Whitetails are commonly hunted by the day. In other words, you can sleep home and drive to the hunting grounds when you want to hunt, or you can hotel or motel up for one night and hunt for two days, or if you have a friend in whitetail country, a bottle of booze and some candy for the kids will put you up for the weekend. Whitetail hunting is the least guided big-game hunting—by professional guides, that is. The animal is good sized, cunning, proud, pretty, good eating, and it gives hunters more to talk about all year than any five other big-game animals.

Even though whitetail hunters are, percentagewise, the least successful of all big-game hunters, they are the happiest. Actual success may run as low as 12 to 14 percent, but morale runs almost 100 percent. One man's comment: "I've never got one, but I see a lot." The desire to hunt big game is certainly inherited from our ancestors, who did it because of necessity. Put this desire together with a plentiful big-game animal, and you've set the stage ideally.

Most of the deer hunters figure they do not need any specialized equipment. Take the firearm for instance. Outside of the outlawed low-power small-bore rifle, anything will kill a deer. Shotgunners are deadly with their buckshot or 1-ounce punkin' balls; the .375 magnum will also kill a deer (even if you hit him in the hams).

Deer are stationary targets a lot of the time, so you don't have to be a terrific shot.

Footwear doesn't seem to be too important. I have come across fellows hunting deer in their street shoes. I could almost see their feet colored blue through the leather. I have even encountered a female with high heels and a deer rifle! I guess she was ready for anything. I have also seen those teddy bears with felt boots and five-buckle overshoes when the temperature was 40 degrees above or better. You could see them coming by watching for the clouds of steam gushing out of the tops of their boots at every step.

Pants and jackets come in various sizes, weights, and colors, too. Good sense and many state laws say that you must wear a percentage of red or blaze-orange if you are going to hunt deer, but this doesn't seem to make much difference. I once chanced upon a deer hunter one morning wearing a dark brown topcoat and a gray snap-brim hat. After making sure it was human, I mentioned that it not only was against the law but dangerous to be garbed as such. The gentleman politely said, "Get lost, sonny, you're screwin' up my huntin'. I've got to get to the office by nine, so I'm only going to be out here for a little while, and if you don't squeal on me no game warden is going to see me!" I left, but I never did hear whether he got to the office or not.

Then there was the good-lookin' woman who really amazed me. I saw this white flicking object, so I put the scope on it. I almost had a heart attack. Somebody was wearing a white scarf! I walked up that way. About a hundred yards away I smelled banana oil. When I got there this gal's rifle was leaning against a tree, her hair was done up in curlers, and she had just painted her fingernails. I told her how dangerous it was to wear a white scarf and loaned her my big red hankie to replace it. She said, "I'll put it on when my nails are dry." Then she winked at me. "I'll return this after the dance tonight, honey!"

Another fellow I encountered was wearing a red nylon shell over a sweatshirt. The temperature glassed out at zero. I asked him what time it was. He was vibrating so badly he couldn't read his watch. I built a little fire for him (he didn't even have a match) then got out of there 'cause he looked like he wanted to kiss me!

There's another distinct type of deer hunter. They're the guys who put on so many clothes they look like inflated toys. I hate to see them on top of a ridge. One mistake would roll them all the way to the bottom. They waddle like spacemen. These fellows cover their ears well, too.

I walked up on one recently. Still behind him (I didn't want to scare him), I started talking about the weather and generally made small talk. After a few minutes of this I didn't get any answer. I edged around a little. He turned his head and saw me standing there, lurched a little, and then chewed me out. "You rotten jerk you! Don't *ever* sneak up on anybody like that. What the hell's the matter with you? Do you want to get killed? It's a good thing I'm not the nervous type or I could'a shot you! This your first time in the woods?" I apologized profusely and left as suddenly as I could.

Now we come to the *prettiest* hunter in the woods. This is the fellow who looks like and is the most fastidious hunter you ever met. His clothing is proper for every occasion, and impeccably done. Wrinkled jacket and pants are not tolerated. Wool pants are creased right and so are the sleeves and pockets of his fine wool shirt. I happened on one of these gentlemen one day shortly after he had downed a nice fat forkhorn buck. I chatted with him for a while, but he made no move to dress the deer. Finally I mentioned that deer are easier to dress before rigor mortis sets in.

"I've forgotten to bring a dressing tool," he said. I asked him how he expected to get the job done.

"I really don't know," he answered. "I've never done it before!"

Shrugging my shoulders, I flipped off my jacket and tackled the buck, hating to see anything go to waste. In ten minutes I rolled my sleeves down and said sarcastically, "Friend, if you intend to hunt deer, you'd better damn well learn how to take care of them!"

"Yessir, I'll try," he said.

I was a hundred yards down the trail before it hit me. That dude must have chuckled the rest of the day. I wonder who he talked into draggin' the deer to camp for him!

I visited with another hunter a few years back. We were discussing the beautiful weather in low tones when the hunter raised his hand. I shut up instantly and looked. He raised his rifle. I looked again but couldn't see anything. Then he pointed his rifle a little more to the left and fired.

"Did you get him?" I asked.

"Shut up, I'm listening!" he said.

"Listening?"

"Yeah, man, when I hear somethin' movin' I shoot at it. I can tell the difference between a guy and a deer!"

I got out of there, *fast!*

Times change rapidly. Long gone are the days of the "whole season" hunter. Those one-room hunting shacks covered with tar paper, filled with cobwebs and field mice for fifty-one weeks out of the year are disappearing from the American deer hunting scene. The ritual of getting the place habitable has been lost. It generally took at least a day of airing and cleaning to please the least fastidious of the crew. Wood was always cut a year in advance so it would dry. I remember the first camp I made many years ago as a lad. After throwing my duffel on one of the bottom bunks I eagerly asked what I could do.

"Go chop some wood," I was told.

I had noticed a good pile of wood right outside the door, so I said, "Heck, there's plenty of wood out there."

"That's for this year, sprout. You cut it for next year!"

"I might not be here next year," I protested.

"If you don't shut up and start cuttin' wood, you may not be here this year!" was his answer.

I got busy.

I wondered why no one had contested my gear on the lower bunk. I thought I had really been treated royally. My notion changed the first night when the wood fire died down. The closer to the floor you were, the colder it was! That was only the first inconvenience. As long as you were closest to the stove, you got up and kept it going. If the fire expired, you started it.

As these places fell into disrepair the swing was noticeable. The old camps fell apart, literally. The physical camp deteriorated, and the human part of the camp changed. The younger men took their vacations at other times of the year, doing other things. The older men decided to quit fighting the relatively uncomfortable shacks.

Now we have become a nation of weekend whitetail hunters. Fast, dependable transportation allows a hunter to get to the hunting area in a matter of a few hours. Snug year-round lake cottages and vacation retreats have replaced the old shack. Electric lights, gas heaters, and furnaces have replaced kerosene, white-gas lanterns, and the wood stove. Gleaming refrigerators and ranges with automatic ovens are common, and the best of all, there are inside toilets. Hundreds of motels have sprung up to take care of the vacation boom. These comfortable places stay open to take care of the deer hunter.

The travel trailer and pickup camper are other innovations that have made a tremendous impact on the deer hunter. These vehicles have all the comforts of home. I ought to know; I have spent a lot of nights in my self-contained travel trailer. Those 20-below-zero nights only make the gas furnace work a little harder.

As a matter of fact, the weekend hunter has become a "day and a half" hunter. His motto: hunt like hell on Saturday, give it a couple of hours on Sunday morning, then pack up to avoid the rush and be home in time to watch Walt Disney, or Bonanza for sure. Next weekend he'll hit 'em again.

Now, before all you dyed in the wool (or nylon) hunters come a-huntin' me, let me elaborate just a little on your case. Yes, we still do have the "full season" hunter, and, God willing, may he live forever. I am one of you. I will admit, and I hope you will, too, that I like to hunt out of a comfortable camp. You can tell me all you like about the joys of roughing it, but I'll do it as comfortably as I can. If this means camping on the ground in a sleeping bag, I'll do it, but I prefer white sheets on a real mattress.

Any hunter—whether "full season" or "day and a half" —must accept his responsibilities to himself and to his fellow hunters. He must never fall prey to any of the maladies that could cause discomfort to his fellow man.

It is a well-known fact that a person in an anticipating frame of mind can see with his mind anything he wishes. In other words, a man can see another man as a deer if he really wants to see a deer. Bushes become antlered bucks. Movements in the brush become deer. Anything light colored is a buck's tail. That's how the hunter who wants so badly for everything to be a buck must think; otherwise, how could a hunter mistake a completely red-suited man for a deer, or a schoolbus with white letters for a buck! Be positive in your identification: *never* take a chance.

The hunter owes it to himself and all others to know how to handle firearms safely. Never go afield with a defective gun, or one you are not completely familiar with. Never hunt with the safety off, or depend completely on the safety. Many things happen to safeties which make them useless. The safety is merely a help. Never point a gun at anything you do not wish to kill. Once the bullet is started you cannot stop it in any way. You must become familiar with the game laws. When you break a law you not only commit a violation against other people, but against yourself as well. The game belongs to everyone. When you see someone wrongly kill a deer, remember the deer also belongs to you! The violator has committed a crime against you as surely as if he had stolen your lawnmower or bicycle, and he deserves to be turned in.

It is one thing to help fill the bag, but it is another to kill game just for the sake of killing. I came upon an acquaintance of mine one day shortly after he had killed a fawn that weighed 50 pounds. He hadn't started to dress the deer yet. We chatted for a couple of minutes, then he turned to walk away. I asked him where the hell he was going. "Hunting, where do you think?" he asked. "Try me," I said. He dressed and tagged the deer.

Choose your companions with care if you want to enjoy your hunt. You don't have to hunt with a complainer. He's the guy that says there are no deer, the food's no good, the weather's bad, nobody works but him, you put him on the wrong stand, you didn't pay your share of the gas, etc. He's the guy who, if he kills a deer the first day, says, "I guess I'll go home, good luck!" He's the guy who says, "Let's open your booze first"; "Loan me ten bucks, you're the big winner"; "I can't get my hands wet, I got an allergy"; "I can't walk much I got a sore ankle"; "I'd help you drag your buck but I got a sore back"; "You got any extra clothes? I only brought one set."

You don't have to hunt with a careless gun handler or a heavy drinker; in fact I advise you not to.

Set an example for the young hunter; he's the one who not only inherits our game and forests, but also our habits!

Let's take a look at the American Indian and how he hunted the whitetail. The Indians were meat hunters first of all, but the skins of animals played an important part in their simple economy. It's true that Indian women wore the doeskins and the warriors or hunters wore the buckskins. Simple economy: the skins of the bucks were much thicker and more durable than the doeskins.

Some of the hunters were not so good as buck hunters, but there were many who were good "Tschipethikthe," (deer killers) and wore the best buckskins. I suspect their squaws were the best talkers too. The women chewed the skins to make them soft. Chewing those buck-skins would give you a strong set of jaws!

The secrets of being a good buck hunter were known to all Indians who hunted deer, but just as with anything else, not all of them practiced what they knew. I suspect some of them were lazy, or purely indifferent.

The Indian who wanted to be the best buck hunter did several things ritualistically. First of all, he bathed thoroughly before going hunting. Then, if he thought it helpful to success, he would rub his body with aromatic ferns or crushed evergreen needles. His hunting clothing was stored separately from his other clothing. It was wrapped in skins along with herbs and evergreens. In other words, this clothing was not subject to cooking and tepee odors, but kept strictly for hunting.

The Indian, with his primitive weapons, was a lousy long shot, and hated to lose good arrows that might take half a day to make, so he had to get in close and make the first shot count. There were times when the Indians used disguises, such as a deer robe with the hair on and a set of antlers affixed to his head. I strongly advise against this in our modern age, however, unless you have taken out a multithousand dollar life insurance, and want your heirs to cash it quickly!

Mainly the Indian was knowledgeable about buck habits and had patience, which is the key word in all whitetail hunting. After all, if he fouled up, he would go hungry, so he was a careful hunter. The Indian did not try to run a deer to death. He knew better!

The Indians also hunted together very well. Many, many hours were spent constructing "drift" fences of brush, trees, and saplings. Some of these fences were a half mile long and designed to funnel the deer to a particular spot where the tribe's best shots were concealed. Deer, being rather lazy, would tend to follow the fence unless pushed too hard. Sometimes holes were made in the fence so the deer could slip off to the side—right into the arrow of "Tschipethikthe." The poorer hunters and young "learners" were the ones who, very slowly, moved the deer to the shooters.

When the Indians were really laying in a meat supply for the winter, the squaws also played an important part. The drift fences would be constructed so as to end at a lake where the deer would take to the water, only to be killed by club-wielding squaws in canoes manned by strong young braves.

When the Indians acquired muskets they still used the drift fences extensively with much greater success. White market hunters caught on quickly, and I suppose many an Indian was disappointed to arrive at his favorite stand and find another hunter had beat him to it.

The Indian, unlike the white man, preferred to hunt deer before the snows really set in. His biggest hunts were just before the lake froze and the snows fell. The Indian knew if he could see the deer further away because of snow, the deer could also spot him. Also, it was more difficult for the red man to stay warm enough in his primitive clothing to become a good stander. The Indian was a "bare ground" hunter, and an excellent tracker. His wants were governed by necessity rather than entertainment or sport.

The Indian's taste buds also differed considerably from mine. Deer testicles were relished for their aphrodisiac powers, as were portions of powdered antler. The brains were awarded to the less bright hunters in the hopes they would retain some of old whitetail's wisdom. Vegetation was removed from the deer's first stomach and relished for its "tangy" taste. Venison tallow was mixed with berries and corn, to be eaten cold on the trail. No wonder the Indians said "UGH."

2. The Animal

The Mayflowers wave their delicate pink-white petals at every vagrant bee that buzzes softly in the warm spring sun. Hickory leaves are big as a fox squirrel's ear, and it seems as though a hundred various shades of green catch your eye. The ruffed grouse drums his love song on a big log, while the soft warm breeze hints at the moisture increase in the air. Building cumulus clouds foretell another spring shower, which will create another magical change in the greenery. The doe flicks her tail, brushing the mosquitoes off her puffy rear. Then a sudden twinge in her swollen abdomen makes her nervous and edgy. She feels a sudden urgency and heads for one of the ever-close thickets as a flickering fork of lightning zips overhead. While the rumble of thunder and the huge rain drops quiver the new leaves, the doe lies down in response to the exquisite pain of birthing. In ten minutes a glistening reddish-brown-and-white buck fawn gasps at the suddenness of the wet air. Shortly after, he is joined by a sister. The doe sets about licking them clean, finding it easy with the soft warm rain falling. After lying down again and allowing the fawns to nurse for a few minutes she leaves the scene. The fawns struggle for fifty feet or so before she puts them down. Knowing the fawns are virtually scentless, the doe heads for a cool drink and fresh greens. She will return within the hour.

Life begins as a small package of about 5 to 7 pounds for a whitetail deer. Multiple births are very common, the majority being twins. After their first fawn, most healthy does produce twins. Occasionally triplets are born, but this is not the rule. In areas overpopulated by deer and in areas where food is a problem, nature compensates by producing only single births. The areas that have low-to-medium populations and the areas with good feed produce the most fawns. Mild winters ensure a good survival of healthy fawns, as the does come through strong and healthy.

Rough winters take the does down at that critical time—February and March—when the embryos are about half grown. Recovery is slow, and the unborn are affected. However, if given a chance the does come back rapidly and by fawning time will have put a lot of the lost flesh back on.

Fawns prosper rapidly. Does' milk is very rich and nourishing; in fact, it is three times richer than Guernsey cow's milk. In a week a fawn can outrun a man. I've tried to catch so-called "tame" fawns for shipment, but they are *fast!* Fawns are taught immediately to respect adult authority. When Momma has them stay put, they remain motionless for long periods. Nature provides them with a virtually odorless body and a spotted coat that is difficult to beat for camouflage in a sun-spotted or dappled shade surrounding.

The gestation period is about 207 days, or about six and three-quarters to seven months. The earliest breeding takes place some time in October, which means the early fawns are born in May. The doe doesn't have any particular hiding place to drop her offspring. When the time comes, she picks out a well-forested or brushy place and gives birth. Often in river-bottom areas the doe will swim to an island to have her fawns, thereby putting a water barrier between fawns and predators. She hides her fawns expertly and will not visit them except at feeding time.

At about five weeks or so the fawns begin to travel constantly with their mother. Their spots don't fade until about three months. Weaning begins in earnest at three and a half to four months, but some permissive does permit nursing until six or seven months.

At four to five months the buck fawns develop roughened growths on the parietal bones of the skull. These are not actual antlers, but the bases or pedicles from which the antlers will grow. These deer are commonly called button bucks.

A whitetail's learning begins at birth and continues until death, some 12 to 18 years later. When the fawns are able to move around a bit they become bullheaded and want to do things for themselves. Sometimes they don't want to stay or pay attention. If the doe can't glare the fawn into submission, she will force it to lie down by either pushing it down with her forefoot, or by straddling and literally pressing it to earth with her brisket. The kid soon gets the message, stays put, and, believe me, does not move until the mother returns. At this stage of life the fawn is also taught that the front-foot stomp, a sharp rap on the ground, is a warning that some unidentified, possible danger is near. All senses must become alert until a positive identification is made or the possible danger moves off. The blow or snort is a violent exhalation of air through the nostrils. This whistling of air cut short, sounds weird to us humans and will carry for at least a quarter of a mile. It tells all deerdom that something is radically wrong in the area, and to be prepared to clear out *now!* The tail, or flag, up is not necessarily a sign of danger, but more of a beacon for other deer, especially fawns, to follow. In the deep thickets and heavy brush it would be very easy for the fawn to lose sight of Momma, but the big, waving, white beacon is easy to see. When a deer wants to sneak, the tail is clamped down.

It is commonly believed that deer do not use any vocal means of communication. This is far from the truth. Fawns often bleat for their mothers with a voice much like a lamb's. Older deer do not often bleat unless they are injured, terrified, or trapped. When they do bleat, it is generally quite loud and the sound carries. A mature buck in the full rut very often grunts quite audibly, much like a pig.

The fawns learn quickly and become very adept at the art of skulking or beating around the bush. They have already learned to lie quietly and let danger go by.

The deer's nose is the most refined organ nature ever developed. At an early age the deer learns the world is full of different odors, some good, some indifferent, some bad. Once a smell is registered in a deer's head, it stays there. The deer may not always know exactly what an object is by looking at it or by hearing it, but when he smells something, recognition is instantaneous.

The gland that leaves the deer's own scent is located between the toes. It's called the interdigital gland. The next time you kill a deer, spread the toes and dig in with your finger. You will find a waxy substance with a strong odor.

If the fawn strays, the doe quickly finds it by trailing like a hound. This works the other way around also. A lost fawn will track its momma in a panic. I remember getting between a doe and her fawn. I saw the doe run down a fence line when I appeared. She looked back a couple of times, so I thought there must be a fawn. I ran to the fence line and stood. In a few minutes the fawn came up the line with its nose glued to the ground, giving a little bleat occasionally. When the fawn passed me, it was so close I could have touched it. The doe obviously hadn't catalogued the fawn with human scent as yet. The fawns learn a great deal about scents all by themselves, of course, but the real danger scents are indelibly impressed on the fawns by the does. In other words, every time a deer smells a human being, or any one of the scents that could be associated with human beings, the deer becomes alert and passes this feeling on to the fawn.

When a whitetail deer is alert, it is an unapproachable animal. Deer do not often make errors when alerted. It doesn't make any difference how still you stand. If a deer approaches from downwind and scents you, chances are you will never see the animal. Even on still days, remain in one spot long enough and your scent will ooze from you like a puddle for a distance of up to 100 feet! This may sound farfetched, but even a human nose can detect odors, such as a dead creature on a still day, at a distance of 20 to 30 feet. I cannot emphasize too strongly the ability of a deer to detect alien things with its nose. If you can remember this, it will help later when we discuss methods of hunting.

Mrs. Effie Kingren, of Douglas County in Wisconsin, relates how a deer named Patty, which she raised from an orphan, used her nose. The deer and a dog were raised together. The dog was killed on the road. Mrs. Kingren had the dog buried but kept the collar in a chest of drawers. Mrs. Kingren started to clean the chest one day while Patty was in the house. The deer came over and stood looking in one drawer. Mrs. Kingren tried to move her out of the way, but the deer kept sniffing and crying a little. Mrs. Kingren discovered the dog's collar there. The dog had been dead three years, but Patty recognized the scent that was still there. Mrs. Kingren calls Patty "radar nose." She says if she bakes an apple pie Patty can smell it a mile away and will be at the house within minutes.

The area where you dress your deer will be avoided by other deer for some time, so, if you are lucky and want to try for another, pick an area at least a hundred yards from your last kill.

I have often seen deer threading their way through hunters via brush patches like a small boy crossing a creek, leaping from one stone to another. The deer will sneak from one safe area to another by using their super sense of smell.

A deer has no difficulty finding a single acorn under

18 inches of snow. No deer paws indiscriminately for acorns or corn; they just don't have snow-shoveling equipment! I have often watched deer in heavy snow, with noses half an inch off the snow, covering the area like a mine detector. When the nose stops, the pawing begins. In a very short time the acorn or corn is uncovered and eaten. A whitetail relies on his nose never fooling him, so you'll have to disguise your odor if you want to get by his most astute alarm system.

Second among the senses deer have going for them is their hearing. A deer is able to hear noises at great distances, but so is a human being. It is the ability to distinguish which noises are bad and which ones aren't that the deer depends on for safety. The fawns learn very early that the constant snapping of twigs and branches is not a normal woods tone, and when they hear this they should be alert. The woods are full of noises all the time, so it is a matter of deciphering which ones could be bad.

My wife and I have spent many days testing the sounds that spook deer. Heading the list for natural sounds has to be the cracking of branches. Try it yourself in the off season. Shuffling your feet, rattling leaves, or even talking in a very low voice doesn't really jar a deer like a snapping twig or branch will. I have seen deer become alerted at 80 yards by the snapping of a quarter-inch twig!

The slamming of a car door tops the "other than woods" list, probably because the sound carries so far. Any metallic sounds—the "tink" of a cigarette lighter or the clink of shells banging together—are bad. The whitetail apparently doesn't fear gunshots, but the working of a gun action will put him into a panic.

The human voice reacts on deer in different ways. One thing is certain: when a deer hears a human voice, he knows what it is just as surely as you know what a siren is. How the deer will react is completely unpredictable. Sometimes they will bolt immediately; other times they will disappear like a wisp of smoke in a strong wind. One thing a deer knows for sure—no animal other than man is capable of coughing, talking, singing, or shouting. If you can't resign yourself to being quiet, just figure on seeing a lot less deer!

Squirrels break twigs and shuffle leaves, but not constantly. Deer themselves are not normally noiseless. They too shuffle leaves and brush against brush and twigs. Occasionally a deer will break branches, but not often in a normal situation. When a big old buck is really disturbed, he will sound like a tank going through the woods, which in turn alarms all other deer within hearing. The deer's ears are able to pinpoint sounds with radar accuracy. You will probably have noticed how whitetails swivel their ears from front to rear. When the ears continuously turn, the deer has not pinpointed the noise. When one ear stops and the other still goes, the deer has pinpointed one sound and is trying to pick up another. When both ears point in one direction, the fix has been established. After tracking a sound or noise that is going to go on by him and not come close enough to cause trouble, a deer will stay put and let the danger pass. A noise moving steadily in one direction is easy to avoid.

I have often heard it said that deer have poor eyesight and depend mainly on nose and hearing for survival. Nothing could be farther from the truth. A deer's eyesight is excellent. I will agree that deer have some difficulty seeing things that are motionless, but so do you and I. I have had deer panic at the mere blink of my eyes.

The deer uses his eyes as a final determining factor

where visible danger is concerned. The tiniest movement tells him what he needs to know. A deer can detect movement quicker than a human can. After all, a deer is not always downwind of everything, nor does all danger make noise. Eyesight, then, must be very important. Deer are quick to notice foreign things in their bailiwick. They get to know every tree and shrub in their limited range. If there is a strange tree or bush they haven't seen before, they will be quick to notice and avoid it until the proper scrutiny is given.

Any hunter who sits on his stand, swivels his head like a radar antenna, or smokes constantly, is giving the deer a big break. It's not the smoke as much as the hand movement involved, although I have seen deer spooked by such little things as the sight of a man's breath on a below-zero day. If you think sight isn't important, try to figure how long a deer would survive if blind!

A man's erect bearing is a deer's great asset for recognizance. Nothing else in the woods walks 5 to 6 feet tall, swings its arms, has big feet that crackle and break everything under them, has a white face sometimes with shiny things covering his eyes, travels in a straight line, and smells to high heaven.

However, a man backed up against a tree, as motionless as he can get, loses his identity.

If you think man's sight is superior to a whitetail's, stop to consider how many times, even with his ability to distinguish color—which a deer cannot—a man has walked past you on a deer stand and didn't know you were there. I have had this happen to me many, many times. In fact there have been occasions when men have come within 50 feet of me and plunked down on a stand until I discreetly coughed so they would know I was there.

A deer has a finely tuned body mechanism with tremendously hard, springy muscles. Fawns and yearlings commonly jump over each other while playing their games. A mature deer can clear an 8-foot fence from a standing start if it so desires. A deer's reactions are so immediate they are unbelievable at times. I have seen a deer swap ends so fast I thought there must be two deer!

Deer not only have the ability to jump high and turn quickly, but they also are able to crawl on their bellies at a pace that would put you to a trot just to keep up. Deer are so agile they can go through brush that would stop you cold. A deer's shoulders are only connected to its body by muscle tissue. This makes for great resiliency and springy turning ability.

Water doesn't present any problem for deer. They're excellent swimmers and love it. I have seen deer swim across some fairly large lakes just for kicks. When pressured, a deer takes to the water readily. Their hollow, buoyant hair helps keep them afloat. The one real bugaboo is ice. Hard hooves make it almost impossible for deer to get up once they go down on glare ice, especially if they are nervous.

Whitetails do not care to run long distances, as mule deer or elk will, but a mature whitetail will run a mile or more if he has to. A deer can really turn on the speed. When they are badly shaken they seem to get very low, very long, and flow rather than run. Ordinarily they are real jumpers. They like to use their springy muscles to propel them in great, graceful bounds covering as much as 20 feet in a single leap. In Saskatchewan the whitetail is called a "jumper." This trait makes these deer difficult to hit on the run, as they are not only great leapers, but also great duckers. First they'll bound, then they'll duck under or behind the next branch. Whitetails often make a great show of bounding off in a big hurry, only to stop cold after three or four jumps and stand absolutely motionless.

Whitetails keep their muscles in tone by playing games such as tag and a kind of leapfrog. They also run races and see who can jump the highest. The big, mature bucks are above such tomfoolery, but they do run for apparently no reason except exercise. They also lean and push mightily on trees and brush after their antlers become hard.

The whitetail uses every opportunity to develop and sharpen his senses. I would suspect that any whitetail lacking in any one of the crucial senses would soon die at the mercy of a number of predators.

The buck deer behaves differently from the doe. His life begins the same as his sister's, but there the pea-in-the-pod similarity ends. The buck fawn rises first and nurses first. He starts to outgrow the doe fawn immediately. If the mother is ever short of milk, it's the doe fawn that suffers. Bucks even start to sample solid food first. The buck fawn is more attentive to his mother's signals and learns quickly, but he also gives his momma all the headaches she can handle, if a deer can have a headache. Generally, if a fawn doesn't want to stay put, it's a buck fawn. Little Buck is more curious in infancy, and occasionally this is his undoing. Because of his curiosity, he is sometimes the last to leave in the face of danger. Little Buck is usually the one who begins the games of chase and tag, often using the mother as the center or base. He will often dash under her belly and between her legs as if possessed, inviting his sister or any other fawn to participate. In two months he will jump over his mother, who may stand 30 inches high at the shoulder.

The first ten months are the most crucial period in Little Buck's life. If he survives his curiosity, man's hunting season, and the great white wolf called winter, he is on the way to a mature life. In April or early May his pedicles swell and antlers begin to form. Buck then drifts away from company and starts to live a more solitary life. The does are not very sociable to the bucks when the buck's antlers are forming.

The antlers are soft and fed by great quantities of blood, so they must be well protected. This stage is called the "velvet." The horns grow very rapidly. At this point I'm going to change "antler" to "horn." The correct term is antler, and as long as we all know this, you may transpose the word horn back to antler all you want, because from here on I am going to use the word "horn." Everywhere I go in association with deer hunters, 98 percent of them say "horn." "Look at the horns on that son-uv-a-b!" "He had horns you wouldn't believe!" "Gee, I thought I saw horns on it," or, "You call them big horns? Why, I got a set home that'll make them look like spikes!" "I could have shot a monster, but these fork horns are better eatin'." I have never encountered anyone yet who shot a "fork antler"!

Back to the horns in the velvet. It's difficult to realize that in five months or less a deer can grow huge horns. And believe me, I'm more amazed when I think of elk and moose!

The bucks seek those places where they'll have the greatest solitude in which to grow their horns. A first-year buck (1½ years old) may have spikes, forked horns, or may even be a tiny six-or eight-pointer, depending on physical condition coming into summer. Those deer that had a good start in life from big, healthy parents generally have larger horns. (The 1½-year-old buck's horns will be small and spindly even though his start in life and feed are good.) The second-year buck (2½ years old) may have a fork, or again be a six- or eight-pointer. The horns will be larger, but not massive. In regions with good feed and limestone outcroppings bucks grow larger horns than in areas without the limestone. Agricultural areas generally come up with big-horned bucks. These areas are the ones that produce the tiny six- or eight-pointers in the first year. It takes, at the least, a third year (3½ years old) buck to have big horns, or the kind that make your heart want to jump out of your chest. The horns are at their peak when the buck is 4½ to 8½ years (he should live so long!) old. The 4½- to 8½-year bucks are the ones that can sport the massive trophy horns.

Some bucks just never do grow massive horns but are resigned to a life of mediocrity. There are also entire areas with big concentrations of deer that do not have the necessary horn-promoting minerals in the soil. These areas are known as the "spindly horn" areas. If you want to hunt big-antlered bucks, hunt those areas where you know big bucks have been taken before, because you can bet that the progeny of those big boys will also have the kind of horns you want.

In the early fall a miraculous transformation takes place. The blood supply is cut off by a tightening at the base of the horn. The horn hardens. Soon the buck rubs the drying cover of velvet off, and continues to attack brush and small trees to polish the horns. He also convinces himself that he is really something now that he has a weapon. The does, which since late winter had been dominating the bucks by being shrewish in the feedlot and bedding areas, are now wary. The buck will often assert his dominance once more by belting her one in the ribs with his newly polished horns. Even the foxes are run out of the field when old buck appears.

The size of the deer itself does not have everything to do with the size of the horns. I have taken some huge-horned bucks that would have to get wet before they'd make 160 pounds (field dressed). On the other hand, I have taken some bucks with mediocre horns that were so heavy I could hardly budge them. This would be over 200 pounds. Any buck that has to be dragged more than 400 yards without any snow on the ground weighs at least 300 pounds, sometimes more! A buck's estimated weight depends a lot on your physical stature. I have one son-in-law who pulls all bucks out of the woods, wet or dry, at a pace that makes most guys puff, especially if they're carrying both rifles. Steve is 6 feet 3 and weighs 220 in the buff. Then I have one more son-in-law who hollers for help when he kills a spike-horn buck. Tony is 5 feet 7. With all his wool clothing on and a .30/06 clasped firmly in his delicate hands, he can hardly get the scale pointer up to 130 pounds.

A deer always weighs more at camp than at the meat processor. It's at the processing plant where you hear these remarks:

"I always knew you guys were crooks; your scales are 20 pounds light!"

"Is that all the meat I get off that monster buck, you crook?"

"It's hard to believe that the head and hide could weigh as much as the rest of the deer!"

"Holy mackerel, if I gotta split this up with three other

guys, I either ain't gonna get any or they're gonna think *I'm* the crook!"

"There couldn't have been *that* much meat spoiled by that shot in the rear!"

Growing deer are like any other animal; it takes time for them to mature and put on weight. Obviously 1½-year-old bucks are not going to be as heavy as 3½-year-olds. Some parts of the country seem to raise larger deer. Portions of Maine, north-central Wisconsin, south Texas, and Saskatchewan are host to the rangy, heavier whitetail. The shorter, compact whitetail is more common, but as with all other animals, there are individuals that will be larger.

It is commonly believed that the mule deer is much larger than the whitetail, but I have not found this to be entirely true. I have taken a number of mule deer with respectable antlers and age. Most of the muleys in 3½- to 5½-year age group weighed 180 to 220 pounds (field dressed). This compares quite evenly to whitetails in the same age group. I will not argue with those who say they know muleys are heavier. My wife took a monster muley in Colorado a few years ago. This buck weighed 257 pounds at the cold storage plant with legs, hide, head, and horns removed. He must have weighed well over 300 pounds field dressed! A whitetail deer was registered in Wisconsin that tipped the scales at 357 pounds. The heaviest deer ever weighed by a processor in Idaho was a 325-pound whitetail, not a mule deer.

I have been fortunate in several instances to have been able to hunt in areas where the ranges of the two deer overlap enough to have a mixed-bag situation with a party of hunters. In Montana our party bagged four good mule deer and two nice whitetails. I don't believe there was 25 pounds differences between the largest and smallest deer, and both happened to be mule deer. Another trip in Nebraska produced a beautiful four-point (Western count) muley for my wife, and an eight-point (Eastern count) whitetail for me. Marg's muley weighed 190 pounds and my whitetail 186 pounds.

The average whitetail buck bagged by the average nimrod will scale from about 135 pounds to 160 pounds. In heavily hunted areas the deer just don't live long enough to get larger. If you want larger deer, ask the conservation department about areas that are not heavily hunted, and join the ranks of buck hunters. Notice I said *buck hunters,* not just deer hunters. There is a helluva difference!

In all fairness, you probably know someone who gets his buck every year. I'll bet this guy is a buck hunter and will not settle for less. I don't mean to imply that I am against harvesting does. I just think there are plenty of deer hunters to do this while I hunt bucks. I like to chew on good, mature buck meat anyway.

The physical difference between bucks and does is considerable. In fact, the difference is so great that it's like hunting two different species. Appearance alone is easily distinguishable. At distances where you cannot see horns, at least small horns, body contour will tell you the difference. Bucks have rectangular bodies, whereas does have pear-shaped bodies. Bucks run with a rocking motion, while the does are more agile. I don't advise you to shoot at a rectangular-shaped deer and look for horns later, but if you are able to recognize the difference, it could give you the edge on sizing up the shot.

I've heard it said that whitetail bucks grow up running

scared. Don't you believe a word of it. A scared buck is easy to kill, and I haven't found most of them that way. Others say that bucks are really smart. Well, I have never seen one with a large IQ. I know they can't count, because I've used this kind of a ruse to kill them. None of them have ever given me any tips on the stock market! If a buck is so smart, why doesn't he cross the ridge to where the good food is instead of starving to death near where he was born? No, he is not smart in that sense. Old Buck just values his hide above all else, and he knows how to keep it from springing big leaks. His animal instincts and the other senses given him by nature are a remarkable combination. By comparison, man is so feeble he is not even in the same town, much less the same ball park! Most hunters have trouble smelling fresh-brewed coffee after they're in the house. A buck can smell you up to a quarter of a mile away.

The hunter who can hear his wife talk more than 10 feet away and not say, "What?" is an exception. A buck can hear a car door slam a half mile away and tell you whether you are coming in his direction or not. He can hear you clear your throat more than a hundred yards away. Old Buck can hear you breathe through your nose at 40 yards if conditions are right.

When a buck sees a man moving in the cover, or toward the cover, he doesn't bother to try to think, he lumps all humans into one pile called "dangerous." I've seen hunters look at a buck for ten minutes and never recognize it. When a buck looks at you, if you so much as blink your eyes, he's gone.

For reflexes a buck could kick Joe Frazier twice, turn around, and be 20 feet away before Frazier could throw a punch. A big buck just walking toward the feed ground moves at six to eight miles per hour. A man has to jog to match that. In three jumps a buck can be 60 to 75 feet away. I have often sworn that deer melt into a puddle, they disappear so fast. I can't think of anything more graceful than a deer. Bucks (and does for that matter) soar over windfalls and fences like great brown-and-white hawks. They flit and flicker around the rocks, brush, and trees like nymphs in fantasy land, sometimes seeming to be floating around rather than touching the ground.

Man has always claimed to have a corner on the uncanny ability to sense things such as impending accidents. He calls this the sixth sense. Well, a buck not only has this sixth sense, he combines it with an extrasensory ability unequaled anywhere.

Of course you wouldn't have to be a wizard to figure something's up if you'd suddenly see about 500 men with 25 tanks and 50 armored cars coming up the road bearing strange insignia. Well, a buck doesn't have to have many smarts to figure something's up when all the cars and hunters invade his territory. This same deer may let summer tourists take his picture, but let a car full of hunters stop and he is long gone. The farmer may work in the fields all he wants, with deer sometimes in the same field, but just let him have designs on the deer and they'll vanish as if you'd erased them. When a man leaves his own territory and invades the whitetails' territory, as far as the deer is concerned, the man is up to no good. I swear a deer can feel your presence. Many times I have been observing deer while in perfect concealment, downwind, and having taken all other necessary precautions. Then suddenly, for no reason I can see, they become uneasy, fidget for a few seconds, and take off.

The deer wasn't always a nocturnal animal. Way back

when, before man became such a predator, deer moved in the daytime and slept nights just as we do. The pressure put on by market hunters drove them to feeding by night and resting during the day. In very remote areas the whitetail comes out to feed an hour before sunset, and you can often catch them still up an hour or an hour and a half after sunrise. In heavily hunted areas and areas of heavier human population, deer won't come out until sunset and they are back in the sack long before the pink light comes in the morning. The moon has a profound effect on the habits of deer. The dark of the moon is the best time to hunt deer, or observe them. If you are to become a really good buck hunter, you'll make sure you are in the field the first week of the first quarter. If you are an opening weekend hunter only, and like to hunt with the crowd, you may laugh now until your belly hurts, but if you are a serious hunter knock off the laughing and plan your hunts according to the moon phases.

Watch for those times when the whole world seems alive and active. When the cattle and goats are just lying around, you can bet five that old buck is showing them how. Those times when you can hardly see a bird or a squirrel moving, you may as well rest yourself. Deer will move and feed ravenously just before a big storm, no matter where the moon is or what time of the day it is. If you are interested in bagging old mossback, you'll do well to listen to the weather forecasts, and if you are way back in, carry a small barometer. It's worth its weight in gold. I wouldn't think of leaving mine home. Bright sun after a bad storm or a very cold spell will generally find deer on the move.

So far, it may seem that it's almost impossible to kill a

mature whitetail buck. This is not true, of course. Anyone can kill a big buck if: 1. You are truly a whitetail hunter; 2. You are luckier than your neighbor; 3. You are luckier than your partner; 4. You are luckier than your wife; 5. You're luckier than your neighbor's son; and 6. You're traveling the roads in the fall, at night, at high speed, and not watching for deer on the roadside!

Any one or a combination of the foregoing could produce for you. The object is to be consistently successful. You probably know a deer hunter who is always *lucky*, and brings home a buck every year, some of them real giants. Same way there is always the *lucky* businessman who is making a bundle when the ordinary businessmen are screaming. C'mon now—if you have a brain in your head, you know luck isn't even remotely connected with consistent success. These guys make their own luck. In other words, they know what they're doing, and know how to apply their knowledge. If you want to be successful, absorb all the information you can find or hear, digest it, pick out the parts you can use, and use them. I've heard it said so many times, "Oh, I knew there was a big buck in there, some guys were going to hunt him today. I wonder if they got him?" If it is territory you know at all, and if it could hold a big one (which means any patch of brush a half acre on up) you should have been in the area right along with the other guys.

A buck is geared like a rifle with a set trigger. The first sound or sight alerts him; the second galvanizes him into action. I have often been caught helpless by a hand or head movement. A man is just not fast enough to out-maneuver a "set" buck. A doe or fawn also operates on a set trigger, but they have a lot of slack. Generally, after you set a doe you can make a very slow, deliberate move on her. Not so on the buck of the woods. A blink of the eye, any hand movement, any foot movement will make a buck push the erase button.

The buck is a more secretive animal than the doe. He doesn't come into the fields or clearings as freely. He prefers the brush. Now in most states, does become legal targets at some time. This serves to make them a better game animal, as they recognize the danger of man more readily than the does that are not hunted. Does and fawns are easy to take because they are more curious and trusting.

Deer do not often panic in the true sense of the word. A buck may appear to really panic for your benefit, but he really only moves out of your sight before he stops to listen for pursuit and make up his mind which way to sneak away. When a deer really panics it becomes a pitiful sight, running until exhausted, paying no attention to what is in its way. I've seen deer run into fences, bounce back, and repeatedly keep running into them when they could jump over in a split second. A dog-chased deer will sometimes take to a hard-surface road and run on it, oblivious to everything and everybody. I have had a panicky deer pass me within reaching distance several times. These panic-stricken animals have only one thing in mind, and that is to put as much distance between them and the source of terror as they can. Bucks have stopped in the middle of open areas with heads down and tongues hanging out as if bewildered. Then, after a short rest, they snap out of it, raise their heads, take stock of the whole situation, and proceed about their business as if nothing had happened. They almost seem to be saying,

"What am I doing out here?" This is one more small chink in that protective armor of the whitetail. I have never taken a deer in this condition, and I never intend to. The meat would be full of adrenalin and so diffused with blood that I wouldn't care to eat it.

Another chink in that armor is pure stubbornness. Once a deer makes up its mind to go to a certain area, you can put ten on him to make it, unless death do him stop! A deer is just like a fullback with the goal line in mind. He may try an end run around, a reverse, or he may try to come right through you on a plunge. If you are located between the deer and his objective, the chances are good you'll be a part of the action.

Quite recently I collected a fine buck this way. I heard one of the hunters in my party shoot. It was close enough for me to investigate to see if I could help. George was still on his stand, shaking his head. When I asked him what happened he told me he'd heard this deer coming and was all ready. He eased the hammer back and squeezed the trigger. Nothing happened! He jacked another shell into the chamber, but the buck had seen and heard him, turned, and was really pouring on the coal. When George swung on him his gun barrel hit a small popple, and he inadvertently pulled the trigger. Then George said, "I'm sure that old boy was headed for the river crossing, but I turned him off."

I didn't say one more word, but turned and took off at a trot for the crossing which wasn't more than a third of a mile away. I figured I'd have time to beat the deer there as long as he had taken a detour. When I got close, I sneaked to the ridge point where I could see the river crossing. I had just made it. The buck was coming to the crossing at a half lope, half trot that really eats distance. I sat down and when the crosswire was just below the tip of his nose, I squeezed. The two jumps he took before he collapsed put him in the icy river. I was glad one of his big horns hooked on a branch or I might have had a harder time getting him out.

Does are cranky, crabby animals most of the time. They often strike out at each other with their forefeet. I suppose if my kids were as difficult to take care of and I had to pound so much in their head in such a short time, I would be cranky, too. Does make life miserable for the bucks for about seven months out of the year. I suppose this is one of the contributing reasons for bucks to be loners. Not only that, but who wants to listen to a bunch of bickering does for any length of time!

When the buck is in the velvet, his horns are delicate and subject to injury from the beginning. In order to avoid the shrewish does he goes off by himself and leads a solitary life. During the velvet period the buck is very shy and secretive. It is rough to find him. Generally, horn formation is governed somewhat by what the buck eats. Limestone areas are known producers of large horn formations. In agricultural country, bucks get their limestone from the fields. Farmers are putting large quantities of crushed limestone on their fields these days. Horns look half again as large when they are in the velvet. By the end of August in most areas the horns are finished growing. The lush blood supply is cut off and the velvet begins to dry. Most bucks are in such a rush to rub the itchy horns they end up a bloody mess, and look quite ghostly if you're lucky enough to see them. Shreds of velvet hanging down from yellowish, bloody horns is rather startling! The bucks pick out small saplings and brush on which to polish their horns. They want something that will give and fight them back. When they rub on evergreens their horns get a rich brown look. This is because of the sap in the trees. Deer in some of the Western arid areas end up with horns of a yellowish or bluish cast. In some of these areas deer rub on plum brush and yucca plants.

When a buck has hard horns he becomes a king again. No doe dares to paw at him now! If she tries, she'll have sore ribs for a week. A mature whitetail buck with good horn formation is a formidable adversary indeed.

A couple of years back, in Nebraska, a rancher friend of mine and myself had the good fortune to see a good whitetail buck being harassed by two fair mule deer bucks. The whitetail buck held his own very well until the third muley appeared on the scene. Then he began to show signs of tiring. Their grunts were clearly audible 80 yards away. The whitetail was much more agile and twice as fast as the muleys. Finally my friend said, "Let's give him a rest; they're wearing him down."

The minute the whitetail saw us he broke away and took off like a turpentined cheetah while the muleys pondered why he'd left. Finally they comprehended and left, but not before each one stopped for a last look before he disappeared over the ridge. That's an example of the difference in behavior between whitetail and mule deer.

Whitetails were eagerly sought after by the Indian and white man alike. The flesh was good, but the skin was the most useful part. The skins of buffalo, elk, and bear were just too heavy and stiff to make good clothing. Also I suspect the large hides were too difficult to tan easily. Buckskin also had the fine quality of always being soft, even after being soaked in water.

For many years the buckskin was used as money all

over the states. Many men were paid in "bucks." Flourish-
ing trades were built up on a buckskin basis. Many goods
were priced solely on their trade value in buckskin. Even
today the beautiful, soft leather is in great demand for
jackets, gloves, purses, and other items of clothing. The
Armed Forces use many thousands of hides yearly for
gloves and mittens alone.

The whitetail is not a migrator. He'll stick around in a
very small territory and prosper. Some whitetails never
get away from the house. They will live and die in a mile
radius. This puts a big animal in a class with small game
as far as traveling habits are concerned.

Whitetail populations were never as large as they are
now. In 1890 the estimated whitetail population was
down to 800,000 in the whole of the United States. Then,
due to restrictive hunting seasons, and an uncanny ability
to adapt to men and changing conditions, the whitetail
really prospered. Being a bush creature, the whitetail did
not do well in mature forests, and being a browser, it did
not do well in the grasslands. When man started to log
the country off and the second growth came, the whitetail
might as well have discovered a fertility pill. The second
growth not only fed and sheltered the deer, it caused him
to spread out more. It was somewhat like shaking a soda
bottle; something had to give!

That's when the true relationship between man and
deer developed. Man wanted the whitetail; the whitetail
actually needed man to provide the areas in which to live
and grow. These mutual wants and needs lead to a very
satisfactory relationship between man and animal. The
whitetail then found he could also make a living in brushy
coulees and river bottoms in the plains and Western

States. Now the whitetail is found in 48 states, plus Mexico and Canada. The estimated number is now eight to nine million; and they are being badgered and harassed by fifteen million whitetail seekers. It's probably only a matter of time before Alaska and Hawaii also boast whitetails.

No other game animals can boast of creating so much business and dollar volume as the whitetail. In Wisconsin alone the 550,000 deer hunters are estimated to pump at least $88 million into the state's economy, plus the $2¾ million for license fees alone. Most of this takes place in the nine days of gun hunting season. This makes old whitetail a champ in the monetary department, and also leads farsighted men to care for him very carefully in order to preserve the attraction.

The whitetail is a handsome animal with a particular grace and bearing. He lives in a man-oriented society where the buffalo, elk, mule deer, antelope, grizzly bear, and a host of other animals can't adapt as well. He is often born within slingshot distance of human habitation, and he regards man as an evil to be avoided, but lived with. Progressing with the times, the whitetail learned to come out when man goes in. Put very simply, it means that now, contrary to what he was many, many years ago, the whitetail is nocturnal. When man is resting and getting ready for bed, old buck is stretching and getting up. His philosophy: you use the land during the day, I'll use it by night!

Summing up the whitetail deer, I remember so well the time I chanced on an oldtimer talking to his son. It went something like this: "They are the sneakiest, prettiest, stubbornist, most unpredictable, flightiest, jumpiest, lovable, dumb, softest, noisiest, uninhibited, and at times the sexiest creatures you'd like to get your hands on!"

"What are you doin', Ed," I asked, "tellin' the boy about women?"

"Hell no," he snorted, "I'm tryin' to tell him about them whitetails." All I can say to that is Amen!

The whitetail buck is a skulker before he's a runner. He'd rather give you the runaround all day than move out of the country. Sneakiness is his biggest asset. Actually, a whitetail buck can curl up into a 3-foot ball not more than a foot high! Even in a one-acre patch that's a mighty small package. The buck will think nothing of letting you go by within 50 feet of him if he thinks you are going by. If you disturb him, he will circle and circle, keeping out of sight until you get sick of the game and leave.

Mature bucks prefer to bed down in the same area daily. It is possible to disturb a buck near his bed ground in the morning, make a show of chasing him, then pussy-foot back to the bedground and wait a few hours. Sometimes he will sneak back before two hours have elapsed. You'll have to be extra watchful, or he'll be there watching you before you know he's there.

You have often heard the term "deer herd" mentioned. This is only on a broad basis. The deer is not a herd animal. Their reluctance to group is one of the reasons the animal survives. Small family groups will hang together, and the buck will join them in the rut, but the only time deer tend to congregate is in the dead of winter. As soon as the weather moderates they split up into small family groups, except for the bucks, which become solitary.

Deer are very curious, but not foolhardy. Soft music

seems to attract them to a certain extent. They are not spooked by music as they are by other sounds. In fact I have talked to several hunters who carry their transistor radios into the woods. These hunters see as many or more deer than anyone. In Europe violinists were hired to lure the roe deer out of the forest into the guns of the hunters. Maybe it would work on whitetails!

3. Guns and Sights

I mentioned earlier that almost anything will kill a deer. The most prized weapon of the poacher is the common .22 caliber and its tiny 40-grain bullet. In most cases the poacher uses the hollow-point bullet for daylight shooting and the solid bullet for nights; the prime target at night is the white throat of the light-blinded whitetail. A whitetail hit thus just stands and bleeds to death. The daylight target is either the thinner portion of the skull 2 inches under the horn, or the lungs. You see, the poacher is very particular where he hits the deer, and also very sure of his shot. He never shoots at a moving deer. The poacher doesn't want wounded deer running around or being found by other interested parties. The average deer hunter needs something far better than the poacher's rifle, however. The law recognizes this, and all states require a rifle of much higher power.

The most popular caliber used to be the .30/30. More deer were killed with the old thirty-thirty than with any other gun. That is all changed now. There are still a lot of .30/30 and .32 specials used, but calibers such as the .35, .33 Savage, .30/06, .308, .270, and .243, etc., have become the popular ones. All of them do a good job of killing deer. Bullet weight more than anything determines the effectiveness of the firearm. The deer is a thin-skinned animal, so a heavy bullet is not necessary for penetration. A relatively light bullet that expands quickly, but holds together well, makes the ideal whitetail slayer.

We'll start with the .270 for the simple reason that it is my family's favorite caliber. I have always felt that if a family is going to hunt whitetails, it is a definite advantage for them to shoot the same caliber rifle. This eliminates having to buy several different kinds of ammunition, and also the possibility of grabbing the wrong kind of ammo.

My favorite bullet for whitetails is the 130-grain softpoint, or any of the controlled-expansion noses. A hit in the heart or lungs with one of these and the curtain falls fast. The trajectory is very flat, too, which makes this cartridge a point-of-aim load from zero to 300 yards. Zero being 240 yards, the bullet rises 2½ inches above the point of aim at 150 yards, and is still only 4¼ inches below at 300 yards. This means I can be off on my range estimation but still hit well.

There has been a lot said about bullet weights and brush-bucking qualities. The opinion was that if you had a great, huge, slow bullet it would act much like a tank, and you could mow a deer down if he was behind five acres of brush. Baloney! There is no bullet made that will wade through much brush, even the 12 gauge slug. Every time you try to plow a bullet through brush, ask for a little help. Sometimes it will get through, sometimes it won't. Just keep trying! I have had the 130-grain .270 sneak through brush as many times as I've had the 12-gauge slug plow through. I once shot at a running buck three times, and every time I shot I hit a popple tree dead center. That's what you call hard luck! There's no so-called "brush bucker" that would have helped.

Any bullet that will shock terrifically is good whitetail medicine, but the one point that's missed the most is not the cartridge, power, charge, caliber, or bullet weight, but the ability of the user to put the bullet where it will do the most damage. A deer hit through the guts with a .300 magnum will go as far as one hit through the guts with a .30/30.

The secret, then, lies in your ability to handle the firearm. You must know the piece intimately, so that it becomes as much second nature to handle the gun as it is to drive the car. It doesn't make much sense to pick up a gun once a year, shoot twice at a gallon can a hundred yards away, and say, "That's close enough!" Pool-shooters, bowlers, etc. may use a layoff for an excuse—"Don't expect me to hit my average tonight, I ain't bowled all year!"—but that's no reason for a deer hunter to do the same.

If it's possible, it's a good idea to shoot the same kind of rifle for deer as the shotgun used for other game. In other words, if you prefer a slide-action shotgun, get a slide-action rifle. If your guns don't match, as mine don't, get the feel of the gun. Don't think you are an idiot by carrying the gun around empty for practice. As soon as your gun becomes an extension of you, you'll start to score better on the whitetail battlefield. My wife practices during the early fall by swinging on our running dogs, and at birds flying (with a thoroughly checked empty gun, of course). Soon the gun becomes a friendly part of you, rather than a cold stranger in which you have no confidence.

Next we come to the matter of sights. Nothing is more important than being able to have the gun come up smoothly with your sights right on target. The kind of sights best for you are determined by your actual eyesight or the ability of your eyes to put things together. Not all persons are able to line up iron sights, then apply them to the deer without something being fuzzier than hell. If you remember to let the deer be fuzzy, it's not so bad. Sometimes iron sights cover up more of the animal than you'd like, or are very difficult to coordinate in poor light, such as you find in early morning or late afternoon. Scope users complain they can't pick up the animal fast enough, especially if it is fairly close. The point I'm getting at is that no one can tell you what's best for you; they can only suggest. Try them all out for yourself. Stay away from full buckhorn-type rear sights, small aperture peep sights, and high-magnification scopes. Pick whatever front sight you want. With the scopes, the easiest sight to use is the medium crosshair.

Iron sights should not be shiny, ever. The blacker they are the better they line up. Sometimes when the snow is deep, a bright-red front sight is helpful. You can accomplish this with fingernail polish. A very tiny bottle of flat-black screen enamel (1/16 ounce) with the rest of your gear is invaluable. You can apply it to your sights with a toothpick, and it dries immediately. I much prefer it to the outdated "smoking" of sights. Sun glinting off a sight can be murder, but not to the deer!

A rifle must be sighted-in perfectly to be effective. The

simplest way to do this is to get a printed sighting-in guide from a friend or sporting goods dealer. A bullet crosses your line of sight twice. The guide will tell you exactly where, and also the path of the bullet above or below the line of sight. If you sight-in perfectly at the first crossing, the job is done. You must use a bench rest, sleeping bag, or sandbag rest. For instance, using a .270 with 130-grain bullets, sighting-in at 28 yards puts the slug ¾ inch high at 50 yards; 2¼ inches high at 100 yards; ½ inch low at 250 yards; 4¼ inches low at 300 yards. For comparison, the 150-grain slug performs as follows: Sight-in at 22 yards; 1¼ inches high at 50 yards; 3 inches high at 100 yards; 3 inches high at 150 yards; 1½ inches high at 200 yards; on the nose at 230 yards; 1 inch low at 250 yards; 5½ inches low at 300 yards.

For iron sights I use a small bullseye 1½ inches in diameter. For scope sights I use a cross with ¼-inch lines made with a felt-tip pen. At these short ranges, using a rest, you should be able to have the bullet holes touching. There is no such thing as close enough. Adjust the sights until the point of impact is exact. The scope shooter will have to hit the center of the cross. If you are off at the short range, the error will be greatly magnified at the long range.

For heaven's sake don't let anyone sight your rifle in for you! Even with all the talk about correct sight picture, people just don't see sights exactly the same. The only exception would be the scope with crosshairs. You can't screw up a crosshair setup, but you can get in trouble with the post. The post extends above the horizontal hair, and who knows whether it is sighted in on the top of the post or on the spot where the post and horizontal hair intersect.

Thousands of deer owe their lives to guns that are sighted-in "good enough." I know one deer hunter who takes his rifle out every fall, sets up a gallon paint can at a hundred yards, and fires three shots. One may hit the can, but he can see where the others hit in the gravel. Then he says, "Old Betsy is as good as ever." It sickens me to hear this guy, after the season, tell about how many deer he shot at but didn't get. This guy has brought home one deer in the last ten years, but shoots at four or five every year! I wonder how many of these deer were hit in the guts. This is the kind of irresponsible attitude that turns people away from the sport.

A perfectly sighted-in rifle gives you great confidence. You *know* where the bullet is going to go. A rifle *must* be sighted-in every year, without fail.

In a lot of our states whitetails are hunted in agricultural and other populous areas. Generally you are restricted to shotguns using a single ball, or slug. The shotgun is a short-range weapon. The 12 gauge throws a 1-ounce "punkin' ball," which is devastating if you can hit something with it! Some shotguns throw slugs beautifully using the shotgun sight; others are horrible. It is a good idea to mount some kind of rear sight on your old pellet-thrower. There is a trend toward scopes on the shotgun, and they work very well. With a one-power scope you can shoot a fair group at 100 yards, and even manage to hit things beyond that. Primarily the shotgun is effective only up to 100 yards, especially with open sights.

Some manufacturers make slug barrels complete with sights. I have tried several, and they stack up quite well. Groups of 2 inches or less are common at 50 yards. One of the advantages of using a shotgun is the familiarity of the weapon. After being used all fall for ducks and pheasants, Old Betsy becomes very lethal for short-range deer hunting. I have not hunted deer with buckshot, so I cannot give a report on the working of the big pellets.

Once the rifle is sighted-in, you have to know where to hold. In my opinion, there is only one aiming place on the deer's body, and that is the shoulder and rib-cage area. Any deer hit in the rib cage with a legal cartridge will end up being braised, broiled, roasted, or fried. I cannot say the same for one hit in the neck. For instance, if you have an open shot at a standing deer, at close range, and are very sure of yourself, go ahead and break his neck. I guarantee the deer will go down so fast you'll hardly believe it. If you miss the vertebrae, however (it only measures about 2 inches), chances are good you'll never see the deer again! You do have a small chance that you'll cut the jugular vein or rupture his windpipe, but even if you do, you'll have a long, possibly fruitless chase. Any deflection by brush can cause a clean miss on a neck shot because of the tiny target. The portion of the chest cavity that you have to place a fatal shot in measures about 15 to 18 inches, so a few inches off won't matter—the job will still get done. There is no excuse for shooting at the head. Your chances of shooting a jaw off are better than your chances for a kill. What a horrible death for an animal to have to starve because of a broken jaw!

You lose very little meat when you neatly poke a deer through the ribs. I know you can't always call your shots, especially on running deer, so pick the big area to shoot at, and take plenty of lead. It's better to hit too far forward than too far back.

I also know you can't hit a deer unless you shoot at one. Belt him, then rely on your superior tracking ability to bring him into the fold.

A whitetail running straight away is an easier target than a side shot. You may hit him in the ham (heaven forbid), but you may be lucky, too. Don't worry about spoiling meat. A shot that ends up in a ham only loses about 5 pounds of meat. Small price to pay for over 100 pounds or better, isn't it? A broken back doesn't lose any more than that.

On standing deer, select your shot very carefully. On running deer *try* to pick your shot, but for heaven's sake, shoot!

A lot of deer hunting is done in crisp, cold weather. Snow, fog, and even rain are also common. This can present some problems with guns if you are not aware. Scopes are much hardier than they used to be, but they require more care than open sights. When the weather is very crisp do *not* bring your scope into a warm place for the evening. Anything cold introduced into a warm area immediately gathers all kinds of moisture. Any moisture of any kind in your scope will then show up. Once moisture gets in your scope, not all is lost. You can open up your scope and place it close to the heat supply until it dries out, then put a little paraffin or soap midway on the threads and put it back together. I've had this work twice for me. Once my scope got soaked in half rain, half snow. I cleaned the rifle and scope back at camp. Everything looked all right the next day, which was cold and crisp. After being out for a couple of hours I looked into the scope to glass a deer. It was frosty inside! I dried it out by the stove and haven't had any trouble since. Scope covers are a big help in wet weather. A plastic bag works beautifully if it starts to rain or a wet snow begins to fall. I always carry some plastic bags along. When you have to bring your rifle into the cabin or camp to clean it, take the scope off and leave it outside in the car, or under cover. Keep your rifle in perfect condition. It is a fine tool and deserves as much attention as a plane or skill-saw. Do not overoil your gun ever, or keep it in a plastic case where it will also pick up moisture. Don't ever leave a patch in the barrel. Keep a close watch so snow or mud doesn't get in the barrel. If your barrel is plugged and you fire it, it will blow higher than a kite! When the snow is very deep I often place a piece of masking tape over the end of the barrel so nothing can get inside. When you fire, the masking tape will tear away harmlessly.

A new gun should be cleaned thoroughly to remove all the heavy oil and cosmoline the manufacturers use. Once clean, oil lightly with a silicone oil which doesn't thicken or gum up.

A simple sling is also worth investing in. I use a braided leather sling because it doesn't slip on the shoulder. It also makes you a lot steadier on those offhand shots.

Hunting deer with a handgun is gaining in popularity as we come to the age of quality hunting. Twenty-two states allow big-game hunting with a handgun as of this writing. All of these states require Magnums, with the .357 being the puniest you can use.

I had the pleasure of participating in Wisconsin's first big-game handgun season, and it went like this: A permit was secured by going up to the fourteen-square-mile area called the Sandhill Wildlife Demonstration Area one week ahead of the regular season and waiting in line on a first come, first served basis. This area is completely fenced in with a deer-tight fence. Now, before you squawk that it is unfair to pursue the whitetail in a fenced-in area, let me remind you that this area is fourteen square miles of prime whitetail habitat and only 175 men were allowed in the place.

I still-hunted for my buck on a cloudy, cold day with the low clouds spitting snow at me. My six-pointer rose up about 50 yards from me, and I hit him twice before he disappeared. A short tracking job led me to the finisher in a very short time. He was a perfect six point buck, and although he wasn't a "biggie," he is a trophy I will never forget.

Practice with the .357 was the key to this memorable hunt. The handgun is a fairly close-range weapon, but I personally felt that anything I could do with a shotgun I could do with a revolver. This would allow me to take shots up to 100 yards, which I would do if I were in a good, steady sitting position. I only shoot with both hands holding the revolver. I can usually keep all my shots in a 10-inch bull at 50 yards standing.

I have found the best way to carry the handgun while actually hunting is right in your hand. There is no time to draw the gun from the holster, usually. Besides, most game would be spooked by the movement and noise required to draw the gun.

A single-action revolver should be carried with the hammer down on an empty chamber, where the double-action revolver has a rebounding hammer with a hammer block so it can be carried with the chambers full. The revolver is very safe to carry provided you keep your finger off the trigger and the hammer down. It's not easy to shoot a revolver double-action, as it takes a lot of pressure on the trigger and it is very difficult to keep the sights lined up. I don't advise shooting double-action at game.

Practice shooting at moving targets. You can do this by having a friend or fellow handgunner roll bicycle tires with cardboard centers down a hill with a suitable backstop.

Try shooting with a glove on, as a good revolver has a delicate, smooth trigger pull which you can accidently set off with a gloved finger if you can't "feel" the trigger.

Practice with full power loads is the secret of developing the shooting skill necessary for successful deer hunting. This can be rather expensive unless you are a reloader. It will pay you to get the gear if you are going to be a serious handgunner. For hunting I use jacketed bullets with lead cores. Never rest your Magnum against a tree or rock or in the crotch of a tree for steadiness, as the side blast from the cylinder could blow all kinds of particles into your eyes. Keep the business end of that gun in the clear at all times. Use earplugs while practicing shooting, but you won't need them while actually hunting.

Regulations are so varied it is almost impossible to list them. I would strongly advise talking to the law enforcement agencies as well as the game departments before you grab your "hawgleg" and rush out to do in a deer. In some states permits are required before you can carry a handgun to the game fields. Some states have only certain areas that can be hunted by big-game handgunners. In some states the laws are absolutely unclear. You may have to have a permit for transporting your handgun in your vehicle. Being 21 years of age is generally a requirement for even owning a handgun of any type.

Handgun legislation is a tricky business, and we are hoping our laws will become more liberal here in Wisconsin. Dale Erlandson, head of Hunter Safety and Law Enforcement for Wisconsin's Department of Natural Resources is also a handgun competitor. Dale kept a close watch on the experimental hunt and considered it a qualified success in all directions. He suggested a possible safety examination before a handgunner could qualify for hunting.

I know this; I've discovered a new, thrilling way of hunting my odds on favorite, the whitetail deer.

With all the tallow removed, it amounts to this: select a gun that is adequate for the job, much as you select the engine in your car. If the 6 cylinder will do the job, but you like the V8 better, for heaven's sake please yourself and get the V8! Pick your sight with care, then accustom yourself to it. If you pick out your gun in summer, be sure to take your heavy jacket along when you try it for stock length. Handle the gun enough so you know how to handle it safely and quickly. Be certain that it is sighted in perfectly with the bullet weight you are going to use. If you use more than one bullet weight, sight for both, then mark it on your scope adjustment or open sight. On my scope adjustment I marked the 130 grain with red felt pen, the 150 grain with blue. I know instantly what to do if I change bullet weights, whether it be because I can't get one or the other, or I'm going to hunt elk or other larger game.

Treat your gun like the fine tool it is, no matter what the weather.

Cuss at your gun all you want—it'll never answer back —but don't blame it for the mistakes *you* make!

4. Driving

Driving, or moving deer, is the most widely practiced method of hunting whitetails. After opening day when the deer are buried deep in the swamps, the restless hunters band together and begin to drive the landscape. Those who are good at it and know what they are doing score regularly. Those who think driving deer is just a matter of placing someone on a stand while others walk through the brush hollering like Comanches, do not get much more than tired muscles and short tempers for their efforts.

First we'll discuss the "power drives." This is a large group of very well-organized hunters (twenty to thirty individuals, depending, of course, on state laws governing size of group hunts). More than half of these people will know the area intimately. One will be the organizer and absolute master of the hunt. He will know the country as well as his own house. Almost every deer in the country will have been under his scrutiny sometime during the year, and especially the last month before the season. No one disobeys his orders unless he doesn't want to hunt with the crew again. I liken this method to highly organized military maneuvering, it's that precise. Compasses are a must. Maps and landmarks are carefully studied. The new hunters in the group (there are always new hunters) are carefully sandwiched in between the veterans, so they can be controlled and directedly properly. If this were not the case, this way of hunting could be more dangerous than the battlefields of Viet Nam! The master of the hunt knows the escape routes of the whitetail, so even if you disagree with him, you'd better do as he says or your invitation card will be burned.

This group will take large territories because of their numbers. Mile squares are taken as a matter of course. The type of country to which the power drivers are best suited is the country crisscrossed with roads, as they must be highly mobile and maneuverable. A group such as this would be at a loss in the back country.

There are hunters who swear by this method of hunting, and there are hunters who swear *at* it. The same is also true of bean soup. You can bet at least 50 percent of a group like this are deer-wise and crack shots.

Drives are made by sweeping the country like a broom. Standers are placed in strategic positions supposedly to intercept the deer fleeing from the power drive, so called because of the sheer power of a group of men swooping through the brush at intervals of 50 feet to 100 yards, depending on the actual physical territory. By sheer numbers they endeavor to comb through a territory and move every living thing out.

Most of the neophytes consider it a real favor to be selected as a stander. In fact, some hunters vie for this favor constantly, even feigning a sore back or leg, or some other vague discomfort. What these guys don't ever seem to catch on to is that in power driving the drivers kill at least 70 percent of the deer. In this case the lazy hunter doesn't score as well as the energetic ones.

The standers turn the deer back, cause them to try to go around the drivers, or out the sides. The standers in effect become blockers in an attempt to confuse the deer, causing them to blow their cool and mill around. Deer are not accustomed to being accosted by such a group of hunters.

All types of terrain are encountered and driven, even the very sparsely wooded and rather open areas. Good bucks often take refuge in grassy open fields, or in room- and house-sized patches of cover surrounded by open areas to escape the pounding their normal home territories receive from smaller drives.

In very thick or broken hilly country it is important for the drivers to use a compass in order to maintain their distances apart and to come out at the right spot. They must also gear themselves to some speed or timetable so as to maintain the combing effect rather than a broken line that bucks will take advantage of to sneak back through. There is nothing more discouraging than a drive breaking apart and becoming confusing or outright dangerous.

Experienced power drivers often resort to tricky methods of fooling whitetails. Like the time we drove a mile-square area of thick, black brush combined with some cedar swamp. Twenty-two hunters were involved in this action. "Big John" Norton was the master of the hunt. We all met on Bascombe Road to get the word. Big John selected two standers, a fellow named Jack and myself. Jack was a good deer hunter and a fine shot; I felt flattered to be picked in his company; but as we hardly ever held down a stand I wondered what was up. Big John then outlined the drive to the other guys. The plan was to drive in a straight line directly north to Sweeney's Road, which was just under a mile. Then I asked Big John if I should take the pickup to the other road so as to bring the drivers back. He gave me a withering look and said, "Who the hell told you to go up to Sweeney's Road?" I shrugged my shoulders and listened. He continued, "When we get up to Sweeney's Road, we turn around and come right back here. Jack, you cover 200 yards down the road and you, bigmouth, cover from 200 yards up the road."

I felt let down, sure that Big John had flipped his lid. All the deer would go across Sweeney's Road, and nobody would be there to turn them, or send them back. I walked rather reluctantly up the road to take my position. Forty minutes crawled by; then to my astonishment I saw Jack raise his gun and shoot. I heard three more shots spread amongst the drivers. Then the area came alive with deer. A big old buck popped out to my right. I aimed quickly and squeezed. He piled up against a cedar in a tumble of legs and horns. Four bald-headed ones loped by, and then I saw the fork-horn standing 30 feet from the nearest car, about 100 yards from me. While he was trying to decide what to do, I dropped him in his tracks. I heard Jack shoot a couple more times. Then it was all over, and I could see the drivers coming. I had help gutting out the two bucks I had dropped. I straightened up to see some of the drivers in that bent-forward position which denotes dragging deer. When all was settled and discussed, I had killed two bucks, Jack had downed two, and the drivers had nailed two! Big John smiled broadly and clapped Jack and me on the shoulder with his big hand. "Nice going, boys. I figured they'd double back on the first drive. I knew they'd move out when we drove back through!"

It was plain that the deer had performed the way Big John had figured. How many, if any, deer went across Sweeney's Road we'll never know, nor do I care, now. What was clear was the fact that the deer couldn't abide being threatened from both directions in quick succession.

Any stander on any deer drive who does not stay exactly where he is placed or told to go is liable to be sworn at, threatened, or whatever else the boss of the drive might think up. Standers also should learn to be still and not move around, swing arms, or shake heads. Drivers commonly take advantage of these stander faults, which turn deer back into them!

Another disconcerting power drive (sometimes to both men and deer) is the drive with no standers. This calls for the full twenty-five to thirty men in a section. A straight line is formed and the signal given. The end men move out first, with those toward the center moving out later. The end men will be 200 to 250 yards ahead of the center man when the drive is fully launched. This forms a giant bowl when underway. Every man moves straight ahead. This may sound extremely dangerous, but actually it is not. The zones of fire are very restrictive, and followed to the letter, with *no* deviations. All men may fire directly

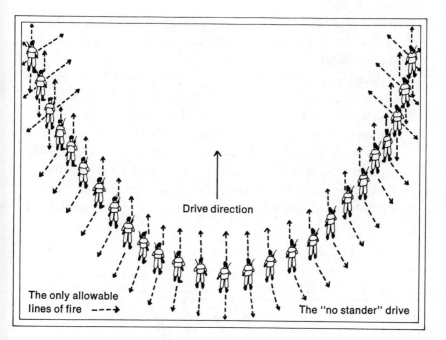

Drive direction

The only allowable
lines of fire ---→

The "no stander" drive

ahead but never to the left or right even a little bit. The two outside men on the top of the bowl may shoot quartering left or right, and all men may shoot directly behind. The men on the right side of the bowl may shoot quartering to their left after they have turned around, and the men on the left of the bowl may shoot quartering right after turning around. This is not complicated and discipline is rigidly maintained.

This drive can be devastating, especially if driven against a natural barrier that will cause the deer to try to come back through the bowl or scoot across the rim of the bowl. The best shots are generally given the outside top of the bowl position. Unorthodox as this method may seem it works very well.

Another power-driver trick is the giant wheel. This drive is generally done in more open country because the greater the visibility the better. Men are dropped off at intervals around a section or square mile of territory. This can vary because of accessibility by vehicle, etc. At a prescribed time and at an approximate rate of speed, all the men, the more the better (thirty-five are better than thirty) move forward toward the center of the section.

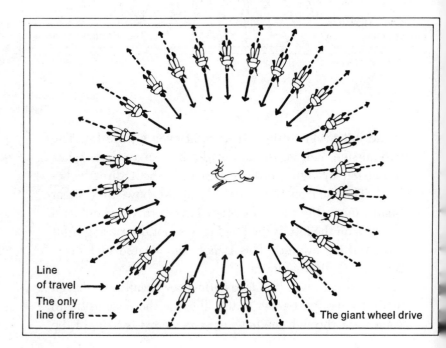

Line
of travel ⟶

The only
line of fire - - - ➔   The giant wheel drive

This idea is similar to, and probably adapted from, the jack rabbit hunts of the plains. The only time a hunter may shoot is after the deer has gone through the lines. This completely eliminates the danger of shooting another hunter. As the noose becomes tighter many queer things happen. For instance, about halfway into the core I saw a nice fork-horn buck go off to my left inside the circle. Five minutes later he crossed in front of me again, inside the circle. In about two minutes I saw him again, loping inside the circle. In another minute the circle was tight enough for all the drivers to be able to see each other; and there, running around on the inside of the circle like a race horse or a greyhound, was the fork-horn! We all closed in to about 80 yards apart. Finally the buck stopped in the center of the circle, exhausted. Big John shook his head, saying, "That buck's got more brains than all of us—let him go!" We all turned and let the little buck stand there to collect himself. Big John wasn't being as compassionate as you think; that heated-up buck wouldn't have been any good for venison, anyway.

That method, like all methods of driving, generally requires the hunter to be a good shot if he wants to collect some venison.

Like most expert masters-of-the-drive, Big John permits no barking like dogs, shouting, unnecessary calling between drivers, or other excessive man noises. Communication between drivers is accomplished by whistles of some sort.

Power driving does something no other drive accomplishes. It gets everything up and moving. This doesn't mean the bucks just fall all over each other to get in your gunsights. Not by a longshot. As a matter of fact, the bucks in power-drive areas are generally cagier than in other areas. The big bucks are past masters at escaping these hordes of men. Once a deer is up and disturbed it becomes more difficult to push around.

Power driving doesn't produce as many trophy bucks as some other methods of hunting, mainly because a trophy buck knows the sounds and tricks of many hunters together and has his own special tricks to avoid them.

I saw a huge buck enter a grassy, swampy area shortly after noon on the third day of one season. I would have tried a shot at him, but there was a thin screen of willows between us. I was on a hillside about 350 yards away. My field of view was excellent, so I figured I'd wait him out and clobber him at my convenience. He baffled me then by lying down. Now I couldn't see him at all. I'd spent about twenty minutes trying to figure out the best plan of attack when, on the far side of the marsh—which wasn't any more than twenty acres and, except for the thin line of red willows running across it, was all grass—a line of red-clad hunters appeared. They stood there as if waiting for a signal. I counted eight of them. Four more red-coats came into view on my left, then five more on my right. That made seventeen hunters surrounding the twenty-acre marsh on three sides, with me on the other side. I had mixed emotions. If that monster jumped out of there and came toward me, I'd better have a good place to hide. But if that old boy tried to sneak out of there, he might just sneak right to me. My curiosity wouldn't let me leave, so I eyed a huge oak just 5 feet from me. The hunters moved slowly and deliberately into the marsh. From the way they behaved I knew they'd seen the buck come into the territory. I expected to see the action unfold any second now. My hands were wet and my muscles tense as I prepared to either take cover or bust the big boy, but it was like lighting the fuse on a firecracker, waiting for the explosion—and nothing happening. I could almost feel the tension from down below, too. From their movements I could tell that the hunters expected the buck to explode out of there at any second. Then everyone was in the middle of the marsh. I could see a couple of hunters point up my way. I stood up. By their waves I knew they had seen me and knew the buck hadn't come up this way. Then these hunters proceeded to comb that little marsh inch by inch.

An hour later they left the area. I was bursting with curiosity myself. I had such a grandstand seat I didn't see how that buck could have gotten out of there. Deep in my heart I guess I figured he still had to be there, although I had watched seventeen men search and poke around the whole area. I went down to appease myself. I still was ready to shoot at a split-second's notice when I discovered his secret. Along the thin line of willows was a furrow about 18 inches deep at the most. It looked to me like an old firestop put in by a marsh plow many years ago. If I hadn't found a tuft of white belly hair on a broken branch in the bottom of the furrow, I might not have been convinced myself. By very careful examination I found enough disturbed grass and hoof impressions to convince me this old boy had done the impossible—he had sneaked out of there on his belly, undetected. I know there had to be a hunter within 10 feet of him at one time or another, but the grass was high, and once the hunter was one step past the deer his chances for escape had multiplied prodigiously by the second.

To be a part of a power drive you must be sound of wind and heart or be one of the permanent standers. It is an everyday occurrence for a driver to make eight or ten of those mile-long drives through all kinds of country. He'll get a chance to rest on a stand a couple of times during the day, but he'll also get a chance to help drag out a deer. The master-of-the-hunt hates to have the hunt held up just because someone killed a deer. You must be able to take orders and maintain strict discipline about zones of shooting. Killing deer in this manner is rather impersonal. No fusses are made about a good shot, or a good buck, for that matter. There are times when no one is really sure who killed the buck, as several hunters may shoot at him. If there are doubts, the master-of-the-hunt decides who will tag the deer. As with most whitetail hunting, 25 percent of the hunters kill 90 percent of the deer, so someone has to say who is to possess the deer. One year I remember of killing eight bucks. The rule is to tag the first one you kill, so I tagged a spiker. The other seven were six- and eight-pointers, which went home with other hunters. Everyone gets venison out of a big drive, as the meat is pretty well divided.

Power drivers are not bothered as much by *leeching* hunters as the smaller groups. The mere size of the group discourages hunters who like to cut in on drives to take advantage of their energies. There are always some smart guys who are able to read the drives well enough so they can position themselves off the sides and be in a position to get any overflow. The power drivers swoop into and out of areas so quickly it is hard to know just where they are going to strike. I know you're going to ask if they don't run out of territory to drive. Heck no! An area of only two-by-five miles or ten square miles would give them ten drives to make. Some drives are made twice a day, so it doesn't take a huge territory to accommodate these men. Also remember that we are a nation of weekend hunters, so power driving generally exists only when there are more than twenty hunters available. Without that many hunters power driving is impossible, so the smaller drives have to be made. This is what I call sociable driving.

For those hunters who thrive on the sociability of eight or ten men, sociable driving is a real pleasure. Again there must be a master-of-the-hunt. Generally this is the one who knows the territory best and is a good organizer. The standers and drivers take turns at their job unless otherwise arranged. Time is not of the essence, and there is a slower pace and feeling. When a deer is killed there is a congratulatory fuss made over it. Smaller drives are the rule. Most of the drives are less than a mile. More thought is given to the method of driving the area. Occasionally the sociable drivers cover parts of the areas covered by the power drivers, taking advantage of the fact there are deer which have been disturbed once and will possibly act foolishly the second time.

Generally these hunters are housed in the same area, so evenings are spent playing cards, socializing, and discussing the day's hunt and how the hunt will go tomorrow. Rivalries often develop between the hunters as to who is going to get the biggest buck and how much the bet will be. If a hunter misses a buck, he gets his shirttail cut off.

Placement of the stander is done with more care and with the hope of more success. The fact still remains that more deer are killed by the drivers than the standers. I don't think the standers realize they make noise getting to their stands, and often the deer are just as aware, or more so, that there is a man ahead as well as behind them.

Standers never will know how many deer they disturb getting to their stands. Often deer are moving toward the drivers before the drivers begin. This is one of the reasons drivers kill more deer. The buck knows where the stander is, so he picks another direction, blundering in range of a driver. I got a fine buck one year before I ever moved a foot on the drive. We drivers were supposed to wait until a prescribed time to get set. The drive was into the wind, as deer are supposed to travel into the wind. I heard a car door slam in the direction of the standers and made a mental note to remind the boys to be a little more careful. Glancing at my watch I saw I had three minutes before I was to move out. One minute went by, then I caught a movement straight ahead. I froze and watched. The movements became clear—a buck with a nice rack was coming right into me. I let him get to within 40 yards of me before I squeezed the trigger. He took one jump before he folded in a pile. I looked at my watch; there were still thirty seconds to go before I was to begin the drive!

A lot of drives fail because of trying to drive deer directly into the wind. I'm sure standers don't smell any less human to a buck just because they are standers! It's a poor idea to flood the area with human scent and then try to drive deer up through it to a fidgety stander.

I much prefer to drive deer crosswind or even downwind. The power drivers don't pay any attention to the wind direction. They figure to get 'em moving in any direction. This driving deer upwind is another reason the

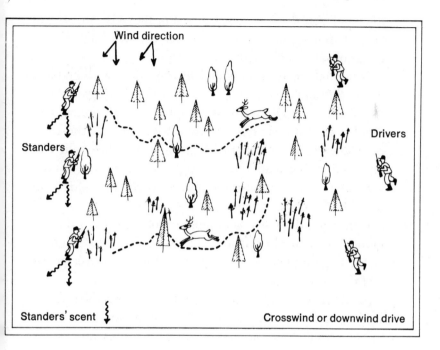

Wind direction

Standers

Drivers

Standers' scent

Crosswind or downwind drive

drivers get more deer. When a buck smells man he is positive there is a man there. When he hears something in the brush, he is not positive what it is, so he would rather sweat out the noise than the smell.

Up to this point I have been stressing the "driving" of deer. I would like to make it clear that I really haven't meant it! Driving is the term all deer hunters seem to understand, and this is the reason I use the term. But driving deer like you drive cattle or sheep is about as easy as borrowing $10,000 from your mother-in-law. I suppose it has happened, but hardly ever! "Moving" is a better word for what you do. You get a deer up, move it, and try to keep it moving until it makes a mistake or blunders into range of some lucky hunter.

Now that we are square on "moving" deer we'll go back to the terminology all of us understand, "driving."

Sociable driving can be accomplished with almost any number of hunters. The sociable drives are, as the term indicates, done with more leisure in mind. The split-second timing, the mad rush through the brush, the frantic vehicular movement of the power drive are all reduced to a much slower pace.

Generally, there is a good mixture of ages, from the beginning 12-year-old to the Grandpops who are still going at 70! Bagging deer is not the most important task in the world to this group.

Small areas are often overlooked by the sociables as not worthy of their attention. Any area of an acre or more is worth trying. You had better have all the escape routes covered, too, or that buck will make it past you.

Before-season studies of escape routes will give your gang a definite advantage when the moment of truth comes. One weekend in the deer area two weeks before the actual season opens is well worth the time and effort if you are serious about bagging a buck.

Deer become very accustomed to using the same route of escape everytime they are threatened from a particular direction. In other words, if you start your drive from the south, and the deer move to the northwest on a couple of trial runs, you can bet at least even odds they will move in that direction next time you try. In areas of heavy hunting pressure, this will probably work only the first day. After the first day's pressure, a deer is more con-

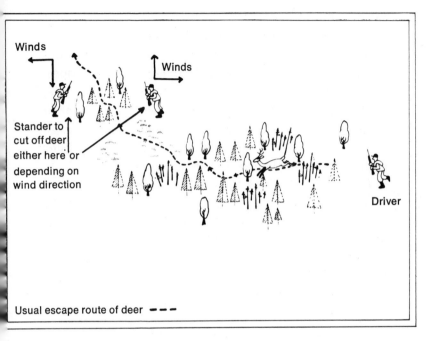

Winds

Winds

Stander to
cut off deer
either here or
depending on
wind direction

Driver

Usual escape route of deer – – –

cerned with avoiding rather than fleeing the hunter. Just as a ringneck pheasant learns to run rather than fly, the whitetail buck learns to skulk rather than run.

In sociable driving it is better to have more standers than drivers. Two experienced drivers will get up and move deer to four standers better than four drivers to two standers. The key to sociable driving is time. The standers must know exactly where they are going and must have plenty of time to get there. No one should be rushed. I'm sure a lot of driving is done with a "let's get this drive over with so we can start another" attitude. If you want to bag bucks, better cool it! One well-executed drive is worth three or four bungled attempts. Remember also that every time a deer is disturbed regularly it becomes more difficult to handle. A whitetail sees people periodically during the year but instinctively senses that pursuit means great bodily harm. Even I can remember when the bigger kid in the next block used to pester hell out of us kids on the way to school. We younger ones had a half dozen different escape routes figured out in short order.

The drivers should move slowly and cover the territory thoroughly. Shouting, barking, and other forms of distinctive human behavior should be avoided. The whole idea of this kind of deer hunting is merely to get the deer up and moving. By not rushing, you stand a chance of moving the deer in the general direction you want them to go.

The day a man learns there are other directions besides straight ahead for him to move he automatically becomes a 50 percent better buck hunter than he was the day before. For some unexplainable reason, every time a man starts to put one foot ahead of the other, he has to have a definite destination in mind. From the beginning of time, man is taught that the shortest distance between two points is a straight line, so in order to reach his destination in the shortest possible time he makes a beeline through the cover. Animals, especially whitetail deer, recognize this straight-line travel as a stylized behavior pattern of humans. As much as man doesn't want to admit it, once committed to a direction of travel he will seldom turn to look behind him or change direction unless forced to.

The whitetail buck has learned that moving to the side and circling back is the best way to handle man. Why don't you and your buddies fool the old buck once in a

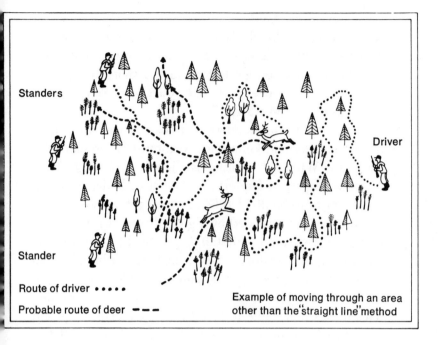

Standers

Driver

Stander

Route of driver ● ● ● ●
Probable route of deer ▬ ▬ ▬

Example of moving through an area
other than the "straight line" method

while? Make your drive a slow and meandering one with much "S" movement. Be sure your standers are aware of the time angle, so they don't think you are lost and give up or become too fidgety to be of value as a stander. Your driving partner or partners must be of like disposition to move through the covert together. Use single whistle sounds to keep track of each other. This is very important. It's not only advisable to know how the drive is progressing, but it is important to know where everyone is at all times to avoid any chance of an accident in the event you do get a buck moving.

Nothing is more aggravating to a deer driver than to

come out to the stander area and find the stander gone or having a coffee break. Generally your greeting will be, "Where ya been? I was just about to come looking for you. How could you get lost on such a short drive? No I haven't seen any deer, it's cold you know! You're warm 'cause you've been walkin'."

Just a note to the standers: Patience! If you want to be a good stander and kill a buck, you must be prepared for the wait. Whitetail hunting is mainly a waiting game. Nervous, impatient hunters are the ones who have to wait for the meat to be divided before they get a taste.

Patience is also needed by a good driver. It is very difficult to overwhelm a whitetail. You, not the buck, are the stranger in the territory. Man at his best is a blunderer in the brush. Being two-legged, man is at a disadvantage immediately. His feet have to be big in order to support him. This makes him liable to kick things and snap twigs and branches. Man smells bad and talks a lot. Branches clatter against his cameras, binoculars, and guns. Shells, keys, and money jingle in his pockets. Man wears hard-surfaced clothing. A buck whitetail will read all these signs as if they were written in neon lights 8 feet high. Man is smart intellectually; a deer is not. A deer will outwit a man by instinct and by acquired knowledge of the human predator. Only men who put on the coat of the hunted can come close to matching the hunted's instincts. Ask those men who spent jungle time in World War II, Korea, or Viet Nam. The hunted man becomes a different animal.

A tired hunter is a poor hunter. He is thinking more of his own needs than of hunting. Pace yourself. A sweaty hunter not only smells up the woods and his clothes, but also runs the risk of getting chilled to the bone.

Small drives are easily done by two hunters—one stander and one driver. Small pockets can be worked that are dismissed by larger groups. Small patches of brush measuring five to ten acres are considered beneath the dignity of larger groups, but never pass them up. I have taken some fine bucks from small areas that, had I not hunted them, wouldn't have been hunted. I remember back when I got my indoctrination to this method. I had hunted several days with the gang. Success was limited to one spiker. After dinner one night I was approached by a Polish oldtimer we called Staazy. Staazy spoke broken English but perfect whitetail.

"You and I boy, ve goin' to get dem bucks in dere bedrooms tomorrow. Let dem udder guys run dere butts off!"

I, being a dumb kid, asked, "How come you want me to go with you?"

"You got car, I know ver dem bucks is," was Staazy's straight answer.

After breakfast Staazy and I cut out from the gang. He directed me on a backroad for a couple of miles.

"Stop," Staazy commanded. "Ve hunt dat patch, dere."

"Dat patch" wasn't much bigger than a football field.

"How?" I asked.

"I get off here, you drive up to dat big tree up da road maybe half mile dere, walk quietly down to da fence, stay dere, and don't miss," Staazy said.

There was a single line of cedars from the big tree to the fence line, forming a perfect screen. I was careful not to slam the car door. In five minutes I was at the fence. I thought Staazy was off his rocker. If there was a buck in that acre-and-a-half spot I'd be a monkey's uncle! The country around that patch was wide open. Five minutes later I gasped in astonishment. Out of the corner of that brush patch loped a proud eight-pointer. He threw one glance over his shoulder, poured on the coal, and came right up the fence line. He stopped at the spot where the cedars and fence line met, 20 feet away from me! I may have been a little lucky; I dropped him. But I was shaking badly. I had the buck dressed when Staazy got there.

"Ha," he exclaimed! "Let's go hunt anudder bedroom!"

Three bedrooms later, Staazy got a nice forkhorn. I asked Staazy how he managed to find out about hunting the little patches. He chuckled.

"My vife, she gimme da idea. She don' like I drink some schnapps. I don' always cum home on payday right avay, so she cum look for me. She always find me in one dem bars in town. Dem signs read 'Bar . . . also lunches,' you seen 'em. Den one time I get schmart. I go in a place dot says, 'Lunches . . . also Bar.' She never tink to look for me in dere! Dot give me da idea to hunt dem deer in dem little places nobody else look at!"

"Why do you call those patches 'bedrooms'?" I asked.

"Hell, dem deer sleep dere, don't dey?" He chuckled. "Ven I got home dat night my vife accuse me being in somebody's bedroom!"

I have had some good measures of success hunting these small areas. You must learn how to hunt them after you locate them. Sometimes all you accomplish is to stir up deer, but if you watch the escape routes and find a way to cover them so the deer doesn't know you're there, you're halfway home.

Two men who know what they're doing are never great disrupters in the woods, so they can pull these little pocket and one-ridge drives easily. There is a fine pocket

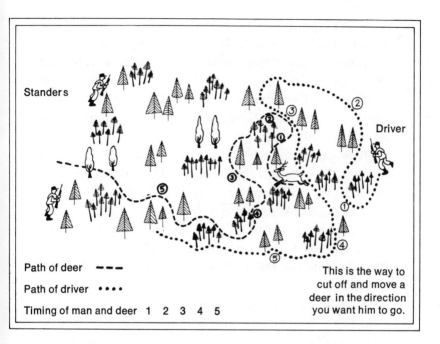

Standers

Driver

Path of deer ▬ ▬ ▬

Path of driver • • • •

Timing of man and deer 1 2 3 4 5

This is the way to cut off and move a deer in the direction you want him to go.

close to my home. This pocket may have fifteen hunters go by it in a single day. Some of them may go through it the narrow way because there is a path that splits it, but no one *hunts* this pocket except me! This pocket has produced a buck every single year for the last eight years. It is a perfect one-man drive with one, two, or even three standers. I will admit that probably as many bucks have eluded us as we have gotten, but that is not the point. The point is that I hunt the pocket regularly and it produces prodigiously for its size. Any area that will produce a buck every year is worth hunting whether it is one or one hundred acres in size. This pocket must be covered thoroughly. It is very thick. In fact I have jumped deer 30 feet from me and never seen them. This is one area where the driver cannot expect to kill the deer. It is strictly a stander opportunity. The driver must try to move the deer up the alley. I never hunt these tiny places everyday. Every other day is often enough.

There are times when, as a solitary driver trying to channel deer toward two or three standers, I have jumped deer and been very frustrated when they managed to cut back around me, leaving me feeling foolish and inadequate. It's times like this when I wished I had taken another driver with me to help contain the deer. I don't have half of this problem anymore, and all because of a smart kid.

There is a particularly thick area that always holds a good buck or two, but trying to move them out of there into a stander is like trying to get the old girl out of the department store and into the car when the end-of-the-year sale is on. They'll move around all right, but they won't come out. After about three hours of being made a dummy by some old buck, I come out muttering to myself and planning a binge to forget the whole thing.

One day out of a clear blue sky, my youngest daughter, who was 12 then, said, "Dad, why don't you go to the yellow can stand, and I'll drive a buck out to you so you can get some of that yummy summer sausage made?"

I had driven this area two days ago and had one of my worse days. If I would have been anymore frustrated I'd have quit hunting and gone home for a drink!

I love kids, so I humor them as much as they humor me. I told her to give me a half hour, then go ahead, but please not to run a big buck by me so fast that I'd have trouble hitting him. She looked at me a little naively, then said, "I know how to drive them bucks almost as good as you, Daddy. I'll move him real slow."

I worked my way to the yellow can stand (named that way because of a yellow 5-gallon can my wife dragged there to sit on) very carefully, then sat there meditating the intricacies of a 12-year-old mind. Half an hour slipped by when I heard Lynn coming through the brush right toward me.

Well, I thought, at least she came out at the right spot.

Then Lynn materialized into a big, rough-coated buck! I was almost caught unaware, but when he turned his head to look back, I got ready. He was only 40 feet away and looking to his left when the 130-grain slug broke his neck, dropping him in his tracks.

I was still scratching my head in wonderment when Lynn appeared on the scene. She gave me a little hug and said, "Nice shot, Pop! Let's have half of him made into summer sausage and the rest into hamburger." I told her I would agree to anything if she'd tell me what her magic was. She said she was going to tell me anyway.

Lynn asked me if I remembered the slingshot I made for her when I was using mine to help the dogs remember I could reach them further than they thought I could. I remembered. She told me then how she got the idea after I came in so pooped and frustrated the other night. The idea was to take the slingshot along and loft rocks on both sides of herself, so the deer would think there were more people in there. Lynn said that shortly after she started to drive, she could hear the deer move, so she began her strategy of lofting rocks to keep him going ahead of her instead of circling. When he started to move toward her left, she "rocked" over there.

I'll tell you one thing, when Lynn talks now, I listen! I have since included the slingshot as standard equipment for hunting whitetails. In those very heavy, thick brushy areas it helps as much as an extra man; but much care is needed to know when, where, and how to use a rock to help the cause. While you are using a slingshot it is impossible to be ready with a gun. The gun must either be slung on the shoulder or set down. That's why I mainly use it in thick brush where my chances of getting a shot are very slim. I have used the slingshot many times now, and even though I carry a couple of pounds of rocks along, I think it's worth it. I am going to experiment more with the slingshot in the coulee country where I can fire rocks a couple of hundred yards across the gully, but I haven't had the chance yet.

Another unusual twist—this time for the stander—was one I used for the first time when a good friend of mine had two days to hunt and wanted a deer so bad it hurt. The first day was a bust; heavy rain and high winds made hunting impossible. The next day was tolerable—clearing and moderate wind. Nothing went quite right in the morning, so time was running out. There were quite a few one-man drives I could make, but most of them required two or three standers. We were discussing these at lunch when my collegiate daughter, Karen, spoke up: "Why don't you hang up a shirt or jacket in place of a stander. You know a deer will avoid that place like it had the plague!"

Those kids of mine are gems! Why didn't I think of

that? I knew of a million cases where a deer was shifted off its line of travel by a nervous stander, so why not a "scarecrow" stander? I picked out those drives I could make crosswind or even a little downwind. On the second drive I heard a deer heading toward the scarecrow stand, and moments later I heard George's gun boom once. When I got there, George had a healthy grin that bespoke success. "I was just about to take a big doe that was coming off to my right when I spotted this one coming from the direction of the scarecrow. When I put the scope on it, I saw spikes so I flattened him," George explained.

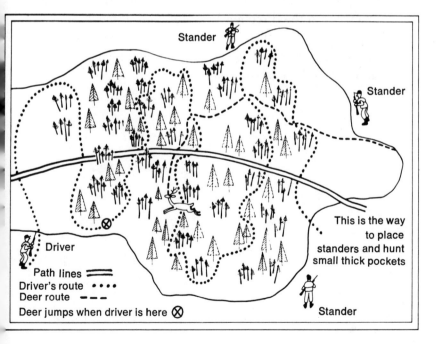

Since then I have tried this several times, but it is always difficult to measure the success of a ruse like this consistently. I am sure it has worked sometimes, just as I am certain that it hasn't. If everything was easy and sure in whitetail hunting, I am sure I would quit hunting them today—and so would you!

The man who becomes a good deer mover learns to deviate from the straight line method of travel. He learns to meander rather than rush. He learns to look as much where he's been as where he's going. Remember L comes before M; so look and listen before you move. A man moving along only hears himself. In order to hear other sounds a man must stop and listen occasionally. Many times while driving I have heard a deer move off to the side. This enabled me to pull back and re-move him somewhat in the direction I wanted him to move. Always keep in mind that the object of the hunt is not to see how fast you can reach the stander, but how much game you can move to him, or see yourself.

5. *Runway Watching*

 Runway watching is an exciting and demanding business if it is to produce good results. Runways are those trails deer use for travel. If you are very observant, you will find the deer roads much as you find the human roads. There are trails that carry the heavy traffic between the bedding grounds and the watering and feeding areas. Main trails are very easily found, as they are noticeable as human paths.

Deer do most of their traveling at night, so these "I" system highways are the main arteries of deerdom. They carry the bulk of traffic in the early hours. Deer using them often travel with that twinkle-legged trot which moves them along almost soundlessly but smoothly, swiftly, and as fast as you can run. These trails are often so well defined that you can direct a buddy to take a stand by having him follow the main trail to the first big fork to left, then take the left fork about 300 yards, and pick his stand! Do not ever walk directly on the trail if you intend to sit. Follow the trail at least 10 feet off to the side.

Sometimes these trails are the result of years of travel. Other times the routes change suddenly, as if a bridge were out. Don't take it for granted that last year's main trail is this year's main trail until you yourself examine it for recent travel.

Once you have found the main trails and are satisfied

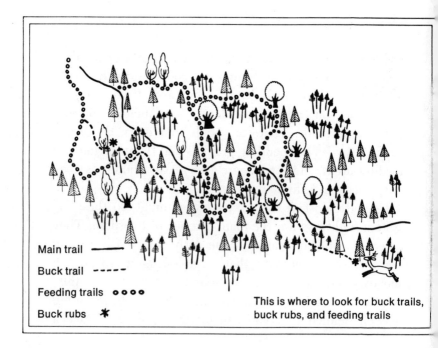

Main trail ———
Buck trail ─ ─ ─ ─
Feeding trails o o o o
Buck rubs ✳

This is where to look for buck trails, buck rubs, and feeding trails

the deer are using them regularly, start looking for the real buck producers, the "access roads." Mature buck are not prone to travel the main highways, as are the does and fawns. Usually a big buck has his own road or path, more or less parallel to the main trail. It may be as close as 20 to 30 feet or as far as 50 to a hundred feet away from the big main path. A little searching will turn up the Buck Road. To avoid mistakes, follow this trail until you find some tracks or definite sign that it is being used by a buck.

I remember the time a friend of mine excitedly showed me a buck trail which turned out to be a well-traveled fox trail. A fox will often travel a buck trail, but a buck is not physically capable of following a fox trail.

A buck doesn't often use the main trail, because it is an open invitation to all predators, including humans, to lie in wait. If you had something to hide, and roadblocks were being set up frequently on the main roads, I'm sure you would start using the secondary roads yourself. A buck is a real cad, and a bounder, too. He will trail discreetly not only behind the does and fawns on the main trail, but off to the side on his own trail. If everything doesn't add up perfectly in his computerized brain, he will fade out of the picture immediately, and silently.

Animal predators are not really interested in the sex of the animal they kill for food, so a move on their part toward the does and fawns is a warning for the buck. If the predator is a human, he might not only expose himself to the buck with any slight movement, but he also has to get by the eyes, ears, nose, and other instincts of the does. If he doesn't pass this test completely, old buck will again fade. If you are going to watch a main trail, you also may have crossed the buck trail to get to your stand.

Your scent may still be there, warning the buck. This is also the reason you hear the hunters say, "That buck came up behind me, or off to the side, so I couldn't turn around to shoot!" These guys often are right on the buck trail, or between the buck trail and the main trail.

In the fall after the bucks begin to rub the brush and trees with their horns you will find these rubs between the main trail and the buck trail. The bucks' horns scar the trees and brush by rubbing the bark off. These rubs do not completely encircle the trees, so you will have to look a little to find them.

The other important trails to look for are the feeding trails. These are rather indistinct trails and branch off the main trail at many points. In other words, these are the "gas, food, and lodging roads" off the "I" system. Always look for frequent usage of these secondary trails, as deer often change their feeding areas.

A buck has only four things in mind that concern him directly: cover, food, water, and sex. To the latter we will devote a separate chapter, as it is a particular way to hunt.

The trails we have been talking about connect the cover to the food to the water and back to the cover. Deer do not feed on any one food constantly, nor do they feed on all foods all the time. This is one of the holes in that protective armor we have been talking about. Deer go on feeding binges. When they do, all the deer in the state seem to get the message, just as the housewives do when a nationwide supermarket has a sale on a particularly good vegetable or fruit. I've heard hunters say that deer are crazy about corn and soybeans, so hunt this kind of area. Well, they aren't really wrong either. If you hunt the cornfields and soybean fields long enough, you are bound to hit them when the deer are there. Sometimes deer just don't seem to want anything else.

In the early fall, before the acorns drop, elm leaves and any kind of apples or apple leaves are the favorite food, with mushrooms running neck and neck. A couple of days after a fall rain, deer will eagerly be seeking plump, white mushrooms. The day the acorns start to fall the deer start binging on them. The corn, soybeans, alfalfa, and other foods may be ever so lush, but old buck doesn't care. All he wants is acorns. Watch for the feeding trails leading to the oak flats; you can be sure the deer will be using them heavily. Deer get so engrossed in snuffling out acorns that they lose a little more caution than usual. They get their noses down to the ground and look like vacuum cleaners. Also, acorns are found under the leaves, so acorn grubbing is a noisier business. At these times it is useless to sit on runways and secondary runways that do not lead to acorns.

When you locate the runways you must also figure a way to get to your stand without alarming all the deer in the country. Be sure to stay downwind of the runways and feeding area. Do not walk on the runways or cross any runway you intend to watch if you can possibly do it any other way. There is no excuse for walking on runways, but sometimes you do have to cross them. If you have to cross any main runways, get to your stand earlier than usual so any of your scent will have a chance to dissipate before a deer comes across it. I remember the time I had everything all figured out. I hurried to my stand. Instead of detouring as I should have, I walked directly across the feeding runway to my stand. Half an hour later I spotted

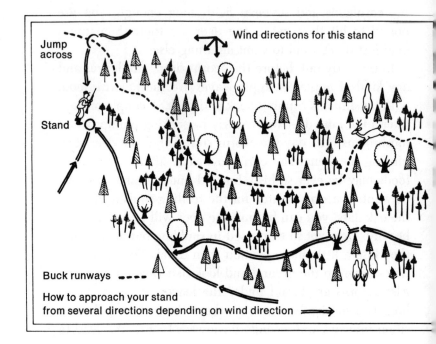

Jump across

Wind directions for this stand

Stand

Buck runways ----

How to approach your stand
from several directions depending on wind direction ====>

a beautiful buck ghosting through the trees on this runway, head down, anticipating all those good acorns. I was about to start to ease my rifle into position when old beautiful recoiled backward 10 feet, as if he'd run into a supercharged electric fence! Then without a wasted motion he disappeared in one jump before I could even raise my rifle. He spooked at the exact spot where I had crossed the runway. Had I jumped across, my chances would have been better.

For many years now I have never been without a covering scent while hunting or observing. I don't mean the apple scent, either! I prefer those scents made from the glands of the deer themselves. There are other methods to disguise your scent. If you get caught in a pinch, grab hold of some anise flavoring and put a little on a piece of cotton. Do not try this with peppermint, because the deer will take off. I don't really know why, but everytime I've exposed deer to peppermint scent, or any mint gum, they become very nervous and leave.

I have experimented with scents on both pen-reared and wild deer and these are the results. Bad scents are peppermint, oil, or grease, any kind of aftershave lotion, most deodorants, imitation apple scents, blood, and above all, human body scents, especially urine, which stays odoriferous to deer for days. Good smells (for deer, that is) are deer gland scents, anise-based scents, salt, skunk, fox, and pine.

A good runway watcher must learn to approach his stand not only from downwind but somewhat roundabout. Select two or three stand areas so you can be very flexible according to the conditions. Know your area as well as you can. The one thing that deer trails do not have in common with highways is that they are not straight. The trails tend to go with the terrain, and sometimes they are very circuitous. You may be downwind from the feeding area but directly upwind from the trails leading there. In this case you would be better off picking a spot to the side of the place where the feeding trails branch off the main trail. If you can, try to determine the bedding area the deer are using. Make sure you are *not* upwind of the bedding area, or you will see landscape and nothing more. You may have to cross upwind of the bed area. This in itself presents no problem as long as you are not too close

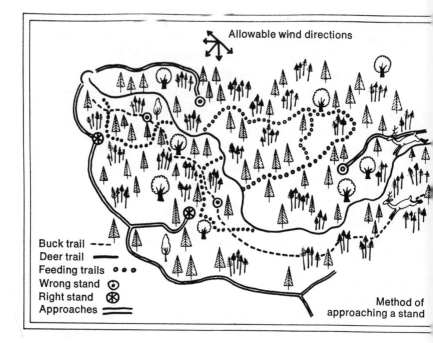

Allowable wind directions

Buck trail −−−
Deer trail ▬▬
Feeding trails ● ● ●
Wrong stand ◉
Right stand ✪
Approaches ═══

Method of
approaching a stand

to the bedding area and move slowly but steadily on your way. Here again a scent is a valuable ally.

There is a good chance that the deer will be a mite uncertain what crossed above him. If you must cross above the bed area, allow an extra hour at least—and an hour and a half is better. I have found that it takes a deer a minimum of an hour to forget you are there, or have been there. There could be a bonus. If your covering scent is working right and the buck is not sure what you are, he may appear shortly to investigate. I lost a good chance by being dumb a few years back. I had barely settled on

my stand, laid my rifle on my lap (which is a bad mistake), and begun to admire the last vestiges of the fall
beauty, when a pair of gray squirrels began to play off to
my left. I really enjoyed watching them, especially when
they began to shuffle in the leaves for acorns. Sometimes
their bodies would disappear in the leaves, leaving only
their bushy tails sticking up like some audacious plant.
Then I heard another squirrel off to my right. I didn't
pay any attention to it. After all, the squirrels here were
putting on a real show. I heard the shuffling again, so I
turned my head slightly to look. There, in the precise
place he should have been, was a beautiful buck! The
fact that he was at least a half hour early by my watch
didn't help me. He had picked up the turn of my head
and was looking directly at me as if to say, "Make your
move, I gotcha covered!" If my rifle hadn't been lying
across my lap I might have had a very slight chance of
getting a shot. As it was, I was the guy trapped! The
slightest move on my part would send the deer into head-
long flight. This buck was on his "set" trigger now. My
first mistake was not sweeping the area constantly with
my eyes. Second, I had the rifle on my lap instead of in
my hands. Third, I moved my head instead of my
eyes, and I moved it too quickly. Fourth, I didn't investigate the noise immediately. Fifth, my mind was
wandering instead of hunting. I just wasn't prepared! I
tried to bring the rifle up, but as I should have known,
the deer was gone even before I could see the sights! It
was too late to approach another spot, so I made a show
of still-hunting on the way home.

If you can avoid it, don't select a stand on a big clearing or field. Stay 50 to 100 feet inside the brush if pos-

sible. Take advantage of a buck's nature of stopping before a clearing, then dashing across the clearing, only to stop just inside the brush line.

Runway watchers who sit on a fire lane or tote road are the worst cussers and most frequent snap shooters of all. Generally all they see is a glimpse of the buck as he dashes or jumps across the opening. Stay 50 feet back off the lane and your chances of scoring will go up at least 500 percent.

So far we have dealt mainly with runway watching on your own, with few other hunters in the area. Deer hunters are a gregarious lot, so let's attack runway watching from the other angle, with lots of hunters in the woods.

Opening day is anybody's day. Half the bucks converted to venison will be done in on the first day or day and a half. This is lucky-hunter time. If you are in a good prepicked spot, and nobody is luckier than you, you should get your chance. But luck is fickle. Five years ago I was really excited about opening day for guns. For six weeks of bow-and-arrow season I had unsuccessfully hunted a beautiful buck with a tremendous set of horns. I had dutifully sharpened my broadheads, blackened my face, scented myself, and all that jazz. I never was able to get the shot I wanted. I have to be sure with the bow or I won't shoot. Four or five times I was within 60 yards of the big fellow. I knew his habits and really figured on hanging that rack on my wall. Opening morning of gun season I pussyfooted out to my preselected stand, did everything right, then settled down to fight off the thumping heart and nervous feeling that go with the anticipation of getting a buck like that in your sights. Then, five minutes before legal shooting time, and just about a hundred

yards in front of me, a string of shots rang out. All my nerves left me. My heart stopped thumping and just hung in my chest like a stopped pendulum. Then there was one more shot and I heard a hysterical feminine voice shouting, "I got him, I got him!" I couldn't resist seeing if this was MY buck, so I walked up to the scene. There lay my monster trophy! The woman who killed him was really shaking as she told me the story. Her husband had dropped her off in this spot and told her he would pick her up later. Neither one had ever hunted here before. I looked longingly at the monarch of the woods while she was jabbering about how she shot him at 50 feet.

After opening day get in the thick stuff and do your runway watching there. You'll find you're quite alone, because most deer hunters will not penetrate brush, but will hunt the easy places. Old buck will get back in the out-of-the-way places and live. Bucks do not really expect hunters to be in the thick stuff with them, so surprise 'em! Locate the buck trails and let the other guys do the walking. Shooting will be close and sometimes fast, so you must be ready and comfortable at all times. Don't be quick to move your position. Even if an organized drive sweeps through your area, hang tight. Bucks are very good at giving drivers the slip. A buck hates to leave a good hangout, so he will merely move around to avoid hunters. This is where you shine. You are the interrupter, so stay put!

Some years ago I was practicing this fine art when I heard a full-blown drive coming my way. Soon an over-clothed, sweaty hunter came hollering, "Whoo-ee, whoo-ee, git outa here deer!" When he saw me at a distance of 10 feet he stopped, armed the sweat off his face, and said,

"Hey Mac, what the hell are you doin' here, you sick or sompin'?"

I assured him I was fine. "You may as well git outa here," he said, "we got all the deer driven out!"

His shouts were still quite loud in my ears when I saw the buck coming, head down, right on loudmouth's track. When the buck cocked his ears to listen to another yelp by the sweaty driver, I squeezed the trigger. I got up, walked twelve steps, hung up my coat, and started to dress the pretty ten-pointer!

Another occasion found me sandwiched in concentrated effort by a dozen drivers. One of the drivers spotted me and came over to talk.

"Have you seen anything?"

I shook my head negatively.

"There's a big buck in the neighborhood. C'mon join up with us. If we don't drive him outa here, we're gonna try across the road."

I declined with a negative head movement, so he raised his shoulders and took off, hollering. Ten minutes went by. Then I saw a big rack of horns floating in midair. The rack stopped, swiveled a quarter turn, and stopped again. The buck's body seemed to be hydraulically operated as it came up slowly and smoothly. When the movement stopped, I squeezed. The deer never knew what hit him. Distance? About 90 feet. In these cases the buck was occupied with other thoughts and was duck soup. Neither buck had figured to run into anyone buried deep in his home territory!

Remember what I said about being comfortable? I really mean that. You cannot watch runways properly if you are not comfortable. A cold, hungry watcher is a

fidgety watcher who'll never have to worry about being
late for supper because he had to dress a deer. Whatever
method you use for keeping warm, if it takes no body
movement, I'm for it. Charcoal fires, canned heat, hand
warmers, gas lanterns under blankets all have their place.
I know of one fellow who uses an aluminum kid's sliding
pan to drag comfort-makers to his deep-country deer
stand. He hardly ever fails to score. His theory is, "Get in
amongst 'em and stay there!" If you must smoke, use
paper matches. Never cover both ears at the same time. If
your eyes don't feel as if someone had sandpapered them
at night, you haven't been looking.

Don't be afraid to use your friends for help. I remember very well one of my good friends, older than I and an
excellent hunter, God rest his soul. The first good buck I
knew he got was the first year I hunted with him. Jack
was very helpful and positively full of knowledge. There
was sign of a big buck in the area we were hunting. None
of the party bagged the buck on the opening, so we talked
a good deal about the deer that night. Jack got me aside
and told me he thought he knew where the big boy would
be in the morning. I was all ears and very eager. Jack told
me how to approach a runway toward the north end of a
cedar swamp by coming in from the south. He told me I
should make it by eight in the morning, and then sit tight,
because he'd bring the buck in from the north. Everything
went just as Jack had told me, except for one thing. About
ten minutes to eight I figured I was almost to the spot
where Jack had told me to be. I stopped to take stock.
There was a single shot about 200 yards ahead. "Damn!" I
thought. Some jerk wandered in and lucked me out! I
thought I had better investigate, so I worked slowly up

that way. When I got there Jack was just finishing washing his hands in one of the tiny patches of snow dotting the marsh. His rifle lay on the shoulders of a magnificent twelve-pointer. Jack had a wide grin on his face.

"Tried to double back on me," he said. "I was lucky to see him just in time."

Then I saw a single fresh deer track in one of those snow patches. I knew now who moved the buck to whom. My next chance came a year later. Again it was on the second day of the gun season. Jack called me aside on Saturday night for a confab.

"Boy, there is a really big buck over the second ridge in that little cedar swamp just north of the big blow-down."

"How do you know?" I countered.

"I saw his track going in there on my way in tonight. He'll feed on the cedar and stay right there," said Jack. "We'll get out early tomorrow morning. You approach the back side of the second ridge by going through the willow marsh, then stand just under the crest of the ridge. I'll drive him out of the cedar swamp. He'll go over the ridge toward the willow marsh and right into you!"

This sounded great to me, so we sketched out our final plans. I was up very early in the morning and raring to go. Jack said we should wait a bit so we could see a little before we started. That also made sense. I was very careful to pick my way as unobtrusively as I could through the willow marsh. I was just about through the marsh, ready to go up the ridge and take my stand, when I heard a solitary BOOM from the other side of the ridge. I'd done it again! There wasn't any snow to tell me plainly what I already knew, but I did see a few freshly turned leaves

that gave me a clue. Near the bottom of the ridge, on the other side, Jack was washing his hands. At his heels lay a ten-pointer that weighed at least 200 pounds. Jack grinned and said, "Thanks boy, I'd never have gotten him all by myself. You should have known that buck wouldn't go in the cedar swamp and stay all night! If you'd noticed yesterday, you would have seen the deer are eating beech nuts, hard maple buds, and some wintergreen. All of these are found on the high ground, not in the marshes. You also should have known the country well enough to know that you had a lot further to travel than I did!"

I felt no resentment toward Jack, only admiration. He was teaching me all he knew, and I was learning. From that time on we made a great team.

Does will use the runways with more consistency than bucks. If you want meat, you'll spend a lot less time getting it if you hunt does and yearlings. Runway watching is a top producer of meat in this category.

In agricultural country, deer seem to prefer alfalfa after it has been frosted heavily. Two days to a week after a sharp freeze deer will really be beating a path to the fields. The does and fawns will be in the fields before dark, so interception along a main route will bring quick results. If you're playing it cool for a buck, you'll have to be more patient and wait away from the main trail. The buck trail will be harder to locate. Look for it along the fence line rather than in the open.

The actual sitting place for watching runways should be selected with great care. The fact that deer recognize anything that looks different means good concealment is a must. I prefer to get as close to the ground as I can and still be comfortable. Natural blinds are the best. Sitting

at the base of a big tree with your back against it is okay. A windfall can be an excellent spot. Cutting leafy branches works well, too, but be sure they blend with the surroundings. I know a couple of fellows who cut evergreen branches to hide behind. This works fine while the branches stay fresh, but if they dry out, you had better get some fresh ones. Artificial materials are risky, as they tend to flap and flop in the breeze if you are not extremely careful. Shrubs and trees sway in the wind, but nothing in nature flaps, and nothing spooks deer faster than flapping things! This also goes for shirttails, open sleeves, state back tags, etc.

The trail watcher also has another strike against him; his face hangs out! There is hardly anything more noticeable to a deer than a man's face or hands. They show up like beacons. A really serious buck hunter should plan to darken his face with some artificial means, or grow a beard during the hunting season. For those of you who are afflicted with poorer vision, as I am, and must wear glasses, you have your work cut out for you. I have been cursing my eyeglasses for many years, and I am sure they have cost me some game. I always wear a cap. Try to find the longest billed one you can. It is very difficult to remember not to look toward the sun without adequate protection. I often hang a nylon screen mesh down from the bill of my cap. This, being neutral green in color and not shiny, does a good job of preventing reflection. This also works for camouflaging your entire face.

I never venture forth without dark gloves of some sort to cover my hands. Deer can pick up ungloved hand movements at astonishing distances. I remember one instance where I saw a big doe come out of a thicket on the far hillside. I had the glasses on her when she craned her

neck and looked up to my left. Then she wheeled and moved off. I kept watching up in that direction. Then I saw something flash. I put the glasses up and saw a hunter smoking a cigarette. When he took the smoke out of his mouth to snap the ash off, his hand movement was like a beacon. The doe had seen this at 300 yards, at least! It taught me a lesson I have never forgotten. Wear dark-colored gloves and keep your hand movements to an absolute minimum.

A doctor friend of mine had a beautiful stand where he should have killed his buck with a minimum of effort. After the second day Doc said, "I can't understand it! I've seen a few does, but something is spookin' 'em. I'm downwind and all that stuff, but the minute I get to see a deer, the deer goes to beat hell!"

The next day I pussyfooted over to Doc's stand to see what I could see. I saw his wool shirt tail flop before I could make him out! I told him to tuck it in or tie it down. He looked a little cockeyed at me, but complied. Before nightfall Doc had a good buck.

Make sure you prepare your stand for action, too. Always clear the immediate foot area of twigs, dry leaves, and anything else that could be noisy or irritable. Make a couple of practice swings with your gun so there aren't any branches or other obstructions in your way.

One other important tip: the second you have a decent shot, take it! I can't stress this enough. There are a lot of bucks who live because you waited for that better shot. Several good bucks have eluded me this way. Nothing is more aggravating than to wait for that big fella to come out from behind that bush or tree and have him disappear completely!

In some states it is legal to shoot deer from an elevated

stand or platform. If you want a real advantage, this is it. Deer are not used to being attacked from above, so they do not ordinarily make a practice of looking up. Scent is more likely to stay high and airborne, too. I use this way to photograph deer, as they do not seem to be able to pinpoint the camera click.

Before you hunt this way, be sure to check your state game laws. Also make sure your gun is unloaded going up and coming down. I do not personally care for actually hunting deer by this method. It is dangerous, and you are not able to move easily.

Do not watch runways from the top of a ridge. I know a lot of you are going to say, "I can see down both sides from the top." Sure you can, but you didn't come to see the runway; you came to see the deer!

When you're on top of the ridge you stick out like a warning sign. Stay just below the ridgetop so you won't be noticeable. In the plains and Western States the white-tail invariably tries to escape or moves on the coulee bottoms. He breaks through the saddles or up the small draws. If you are just below the ridge, there is also a good chance one will come over the saddle right into you.

If while runway watching you spook a good buck from your stand, don't go to the same stand the next day and expect to see that buck, because he won't be back there for at least two days. He will avoid that spot like the plague. Move 200 to 400 yards away and your chances will be twice as good. We are talking about nondriven deer, of course.

Watching runways properly involves a knowledge of the whitetails in your particular area, or the area you plan to hunt, of course. It is better to scout the area before you

hunt it. Even if you have only three days to hunt, spend at least one full day looking over the territory. While you are looking, be hunting. You can employ some methods of still-hunting while cruising the territory.

Some of the most uninformed hunters take deer consistently because they know three things. By uninformed, I mean hunters who wouldn't know a scrape if they fell in it or a rub if the sun was shining on it, but they know how to find a stand along a trail, they know how to sit still, and they know how to kill the deer when it appears.

6. Still-Hunting

Still-hunting is the most beautiful way to hunt a whitetail. This method is actually a combination of trail watching, moving, and driving. It requires an intimate knowledge of the buck and his habits. Still-hunting also demands the utmost discipline. It's you against deer, and the deer is better equipped.

As a loner you'll want to learn everything you can. This type of hunting is also very well suited for two people. A good hunting partner is a gem to be nurtured. Two good still-hunters are always successful.

When still-hunting you actually search out the buck and get into position to take him. After the very first hours of the day, when you may intercept animals on the move toward their bed grounds, it is the time to meet old buck resting on his home ground. Still-hunting must

be done into the wind at some angle. You'll find it impossible to deceive an old buck if he winds you.

The still-hunter probes areas the average hunter passes by on his strolls through the woods. For those of you who think the still-hunter can perform only in remote areas free of other hunters, forget it! Where there are other hunters, all you have to do is change your methods slightly.

I will agree that I like to still-hunt in areas where hunters are few and far between. What hunter doesn't? But these areas are almost as scarce as big trophy bucks, so you must adapt.

Clothing and boots are the first consideration in still-hunting. Boots must be comfortable and suited to the terrain you will cover. If the country is dry, I prefer a light leather boot about 9 inches high, with a tough, well-cleated, softish sole. My second choice for all-round hunting is a very light noninsulated rubber boot about 12 inches high. I know I'll get some argument, but then you are entitled to your opinion. If the weather is very cold, a good, insulated boot is a must. I prefer the all-rubber kind with a 20-degree-below-zero rating, or the new nylon-upper, rubber-bottom, felt-insert snowmobile boot.

Clothing is not difficult. Any serious deer hunter will wear soft outer clothes, both pants and jacket or upper. Wool is tough to beat. I have never found anything better. Wool is durable, warm, soft, and, virtually noiseless in the brush.

Nylon jackets have saved the lives of countless thousands of deer. I can't even begin to estimate the deer saved by the addition of nylon plants or the complete coverall nylon suit! I'm almost convinced that nylon is one of the reasons we have more deer now than ever before, even in the face of increased hunting pressure. All kidding aside, before the nylon jacket manufacturers picket me and you readers burn this book, let me explain: nylon is the noisiest material ever invented. Anyone wearing a nylon jacket and walking is a real swisher. I have experimented with deer many times, and I've found they can hear nylon against nylon, or nylon against brush, at a hundred yards!

This is one of those alien sounds in the woods. I don't own any stock in a woolen mill or anything like that, so I'm not pushing wool for monetary gain. As a matter of fact, I own several good, insulated nylon jackets, including down jackets. I feel they are a real boon. I can well remember the many days my shoulders ached from carrying a heavy wool jacket on my back all day. Now, here's the secret: wear a light wool shirt over the nylon. I can't get excited over insulated nylon pants or coveralls for deer hunting. I believe a good pair of wool pants hung on suspenders and cut to hang about 5 inches off the ground are just the ticket. Wear them as outer pants.

When you wear a wool shirt over a jacket there is one point you must remember: None of your clothing should flap. This means buttons, or preferably a good safety pin or two on the bottom of that shirt to keep it snug to your body. This also helps to prevent annoying snagging of hanging shirt tails. Your cap should also be wool or very soft leather rather than nylon or simulated leather.

The still-hunter, when successful, feels an accomplishment other hunters can't feel. He has met the game on its own terms and won. Even if the hunter doesn't bag the game, he has had the pleasure of the game's company.

It's something like playing chess; you don't always have to win to know you've been in a good game.

My wife calls me a *still* hunter. She says, "You went hunting on our honeymoon, and you're still hunting!"

To show you how unfair she really is, she accuses me of spending all my time hunting, which is definitely not true. I spend some of it sleeping!

Still-hunting alone is an acquired art. It calls for great self-discipline. The lone hunter cannot afford to make mistakes; he must be able to take advantage of the one chance he might get. His rifle or shotgun must fit like a glove, and he must know the piece intimately. The experienced still-hunter, unlike the novice, knows what to look for. He knows he'll hardly ever see a full deer, as he would in the zoo. He'll look for an ear, a horn, a nose, an eye, or even a couple of tan-colored saplings growing close together and straight up. Often I am able to catch the horizontal line that turns out to be a deer's back line. The interval between the first glimpse and the final decision on what you've seen may last several minutes. That's a long time to be frozen in one position.

One of the most common errors the beginning still-hunter commits is hand and arm swinging. The still-hunter must learn to keep arm and hand movements to the absolute minimum. One of the old hunters I learned from, Josh by name, berated me one day.

"Vot da hell ya doin', practicing a speech in da woods, ja? Ya look like a damn politician on da box promisin' da vorld. Ya gonna hunt wid me, I gonna clamp you in a straight jacket, ja!"

Then he laughed, but I got the message.

Man is the only animal a whitetail sees that uses his

hands to push the brush aside, blow his nose, wipe his brow, keep his balance, push his cap up, pull it down, and on and on. These movements occur mostly from 30 inches off the ground on up, so they can't be mistaken for leg movements by an animal. This is another of Old Buck's built-in alarms. If it moves from his eye upwards or sideways more than a couple of inches, it could be a man.

While you are practicing in the off season put your hands in your pockets and leave them there. Soon you'll find you can slide through the brush like an animal. Once you have trained yourself this way, start training yourself with your gun. Remember, your gun is an extension of you, and its movement can be readily picked up by an animal.

Now train yourself to move your head at a minimum. Move your eyes more and your head less. All of your movements should be measured and deliberate.

The most difficult of all maneuvers is walking. Man has trained himself from childhood to move along at a certain rate of speed. Most hunters walk at this same rate whether they are going to the supermarket, taking the kid to the zoo, going out for a hike, or hunting.

The still-hunter must move at a snail's pace. This may sound ridiculous to you, but if it is something you can't stomach, you'll never be a still-hunter! About a half mile per hour while hunting is absolutely top speed. Half that speed will be almost twice as productive. You're going to say, "But I can't cover any territory that way!" I'm going to say right back, "Oh yes you can!"

In fair territory, two hours of hunting could put you next to a lot of deer. I'm not asking you to walk a quarter

or a half mile per hour through known unproductive territory such as mowed hayfields; but while you are hunting
what should be productive territory, that's the speed at
which you should move.

I have heard walkers tell time and again how many
deer they see in a day. "Boy, I sure saw a lot of tails today!" is a favorite phrase.

I am not interested in seeing lots of deer at a distance;
I want to see *one* deer within range. Glimpsing deer
doesn't mean much. All it means is there are deer in the
territory, which is something you ought to be able to tell
by the signs on the ground.

We have discussed the importance of slow, deliberate
movements; now we'll tackle noise. It is impossible to
move through the weeds, willows, woods, and water without making a sound. I remember how smart I was when I
thought I was the best in the world! I figured I would
sneak up on Josh and scare the hell out of him. I was
really careful where my feet touched down and how I
carried myself. I came in beautifully upwind, and was
just about to holler "BOO" when Josh shot his rifle straight
into the air! It scared me so bad I jumped 3 feet. Josh
laughed like mad and said, "Ha, you dummy, wot you
try? You make noise like a rhinoceros trompin' on an acre
of bells! If I take your gun away so ja don' hit da tree
wit it, take all your shells, an you Zippo outta your pocket;
oil dat sling swivel, and clap ya on da side-a you rattlin'
head so's ya remember never to step into a bush, but always around it, maybe if ya practice silence everyday for
the next twenty years, maybe I get so deaf even you
could sneak up on me!"

Then he laughed again and hit me so hard on the

shoulder with his big hand I almost collapsed. Again I got the message!

The idea is to make only those noises that are woods noises. Animals are not alarmed by natural noises. Deer are alarmed by the footfalls of man when he can recognize them as such. Steady walking is a dead giveaway. The minute a man tries to sneak up on a whitetail buck he becomes ludicrous. Try to move somewhat erratically, so a deer won't really know that you're not another deer. Try not to be furtive, only casual.

Your eyes were given to you so you could see in gorgeous technicolor and wonderful wide-screen panavision. Most animals have to be satisfied with their black-and-white sets. The difference between their eyes and yours is merely one of recognition. Man sees quite well, and with binoculars can compete with pronghorn antelope and wild sheep.

You are so accustomed to seeing large objects such as automobiles, trucks, planes, buildings, and other man-made objects with harsh verticle and horizontal lines that you'll have difficulty searching for and recognizing those soft, round curves that nature deals in. I'm speaking strictly of deer, not dear, hunting! Picking out a deer among all the rounding bushes and leaves is much like picking out a blue Chevy in a parking lot full of blue GM cars. You've got to recognize what you are looking for. If that Chevy moves, you've got it pegged; otherwise you might have to look for those three separate lights in the rear to recognize it. Catch on?

Train yourself to look for parts of a deer rather than the whole animal. While still-hunting, your advantage is the ability to scan and recognize. I remember one instance where I was still-hunting under good conditions (light breeze, quiet woods). I had just finished scanning a 180 degree arc and was giving it a second look before moving a step or two. There was a small stub on a cedar about 30 yards away that I didn't remember seeing on the first sweep. I looked very hard, then recognized it as about 4 inches of a deer's nose and jaw. Very smoothly my rifle came up and waited for something to happen. Just about the time my arms were going to fall off I thought I had better push the safety off to be ready. The click of the safety brought a nice buck's head and neck from behind the cedar. He never knew what made the click. As I examined him I saw he had been bedded at the base of two cedars. Evidently he became suspicious of something and stood up. If I had not looked twice, or had not become suspicious of the stub, my next step would have sent the buck a-flyin', probably without even a shot.

On another occasion I had just finished a careful step when, some 50 yards away, a deer rose from its bed, then disappeared before my very eyes. The deer was there—I had seen the movement—but try as I might I couldn't make out any of that animal. I sucked in between my lips to make a squeaking sound. A big ear twinked in my direction. All of a sudden it was very easy to see the head and shoulders of a pretty little fork horn. He had about three quarters of an inch of tallow covering his backside!

While scanning, look over the territory at least twice before making another move. Be very careful to glance down before you step. This is the time you do not want to crack a branch. Place your feet very carefully and try to stay on balance all the time. A glance now and then at the ground a little ahead of you will keep you from trapping yourself in a spot full of dry branches. Notice that I use the word *glance* rather than *look*. The only time you'll see a deer lying at your feet is after you've killed him! Keep your eyes ahead, looking all around, 99 percent of the time. That's where the game is. Don't forget to swing behind you constantly. Deer may let you go by, then try to sneak out. Also, a deer may approach you from the rear. A buck will, on rare occasions, actually trail you—especially if you happen to be wearing a good gland scent. Do not exceed the half mile per hour speed limit and you won't sweat and increase your man scent.

I have had bucks follow me several times. A couple of years ago we had a beautiful summery opening day. As a matter of fact, it was more like bullfrog huntin' weather than deer season. The animals were not moving at all, so I decided to go in after them. It had rained about an inch the night before. The day was almost breezeless, so the woods were pretty damp, quiet and ideal for still-hunting. I headed for the heavy brush because I knew this is where the bucks would be. Other hunters were all around, but none of them would tackle the heavy stuff. I worked my way very slowly through the thickets. In about an hour I came to an uprooted tree and decided to walk up the big trunk and sit a while. It was hot creeping through that brush. I was there about 15 minutes when there was a movement from where I had come. It was a perfect setup. My stand was about 8 feet off the ground and I could see quite well. A nice round six-pointer was actually on my trail! I was dosed up with gland scent, but I'm sure I must have left some human scent also. As long as I had the advantage I decided to let him come. He seemed very perplexed. He would put his nose to the ground, move a couple of steps, then look very intently ahead, as if to say, "That's funny, that guy must be following one of my broads!"

I let him get just 30 feet away before I raised my rifle. I had been so intent on watching the buck that I had neglected to push off the safety. When I did, the buck looked up in wonderment, as if to say, "How did you get up there?" His hide is one of those in my fall shirt!

Many times deer can be coaxed into moving or showing themselves. There are a lot of times I don't believe my eyes 100 percent. When you think you have seen a movement, stick with it; it could pay off. A standoff when you can't really find any proof that satisfies you, can sometimes be broken by using the squeak I mentioned before. It's the same thing basically that you do to get a baby's attention or make him laugh. Suck in, between pursed lips, and make a squeaking sound. This should get you at least an ear movement. Sometimes it gets you a whole head movement, or a tail flick.

I have also gotten good response to a foot movement in the grass or leaves to make noise. Do not move your leg, just your foot.

A sure result-getter is a whistle. It is almost too sure. An old buck may be whistle-wise and melt out of sight!

Your ears should also be trained to pick up the sounds you want to filter out of the normal woods noises. When you travel too fast in the woods you only hear your own sounds, or those sounds that are loud enough to drown out your own. Once I was really engrossed in still-hunting, but after about an hour I became bored with the slow progress and speeded up the pace to match my accelerating desire to see more country. All of a sudden a sharp, "Where da hell you goin'?" almost gave me a heart seizure! Josh laughed as he said, "Boy, if you not gonna listen to me I'm not gonna waste my breath tellin' you how to hunt them bucks. *I* hear you trompin' eighty yards away!"

Boredom is probably the hardest thing to conquer. Until you are conditioned to still-hunting, your thoughts will run more to, "I don't think this is the way to do it!" than to, "Boy, that buck may stand up or appear any second now." A good still-hunter thinks positive thoughts and expects the next step or look around to produce a deer.

Every noise should be eye investigated until proven out. Leaf shuffling, squirrel scolding, blue jay scolding, brush swishing, thudding hooves, all play an important part in a still-hunter's life. I remember the day I was hunting a thick ridgeside. When I got near the point, I could hear a squirrel scuffling for nuts in the leaves right around the point. I almost started to work down the ridge, but decided to investigate further first. Five steps and ten minutes later brought my eyes around the corner enough to see a flicking white tail. My rifle was up and ready when the eight-pointer raised his head. He fell right in the very spot where he was nuzzling and pawing the leaves for acorns.

As long as you work the area very slowly you'll have plenty of time to use your eyes and ears in the way God really meant you to. Too many times eyes look but do not see and ears listen but do not hear. It is difficult not to spin your head and body around when you hear a noise, but you must condition yourself if you are to be successful. The only time you should act fast is when you hear an animal departing. If this happens, and it will, your rifle or shotgun should fit well enough to come to bear on the animal instantly.

The good still-hunter also trains his nose to be of help. You are always working into the breeze somewhat, so you do have some advantage. Deer also have an odor. If a deer gets up out of his bed and is not really alarmed, one of the first things he'll do is urinate. If your nose is at all sharp, and the buck is close enough, you'll smell it. The buck's body itself smells a little musky. You'll learn to recognize it after you have smelled it once or twice. Catch a whiff and it can alert you enough to make the difference between failure and success. A doe in heat smells quite strong. A buck in the rut is sometimes so odoriferous that you can smell him for a hundred yards downwind!

Try to combine all your senses with a disciplining of the body, and you'll be well on the way to becoming a good still-hunter.

While still-hunting, if there are other hunters in the area, chances are very good that you'll see game which is moving to avoid them. This is another reason to move slowly, so you won't disturb the game yourself.

Go into the coverts with the expectancy that you will see game any second.

There are times when the condition of the woods is suitable for anything but still-hunting. When conditions are impossible don't waste your time. Use some other method when the snow is crusty or the leaves are like cornflakes. High winds make the deer nervous, and it is extremely difficult to hunt them under these conditions. High winds make it difficult for a deer to hear and distinguish noises. Brush whipping around, leaves rattling, branches breaking, and noises being masked by other noises—all of these things leave a deer as nervous as you are when you're trying to set up a hunting trip on the phone and the kids are playing cowboy and Indians with you as the divider!

High winds also dissipate scent very quickly. Scent just can't make it in all that churning of air. Being robbed of a lot of their protective devices, deer tend to lay low and be very irritable. Eyesight is the sense deer bank on most in high winds. With everything blowing around it's hard to distinguish and recognize small individual moves. A deer is more likely to recognize you by your stillness at this time. In other words, everything else is moving around and swaying, but you are not. This again makes them very spooky. Should you happen on deer in this kind of weather you'll find them jumpy and not likely to give you a decent shot.

Your best opportunity in days of high winds are at the very tail end of the day. Watch the open fields, wherever they may be. In the deep, woodsy areas there are always pastures or openings. Watch the largest of these.

In very broken or very steep country, deer will tend to seek places out of the wind, or the lee areas. In flatter areas, spruce or cedar swamps are much sought in high winds. If you have more time to hunt, it is better not to try to get among the deer at this time. You only make them spookier for tomorrow. If your time is limited, go ahead and hunt. I'll wish you lots of luck. You'll need it!

I love to hunt in drizzly weather. Even a very light rain isn't bad. The woods becomes tolerable to walk in. You can make some mistakes and not be severely penalized. Wet leaves and underbrush are quieter. Twigs and small branches are not so liable to crackle. This is truly the time for you to creep through the woods. Of course you must use your eyes more. You'll find it difficult to hear, more so than the deer. Your nose will be of more help. Work into the breeze and keep your nose open! You undoubtedly have found out your dog has a strong odor when wet. Scent hangs better and travels better on damp days. Old Buck likes to get up and move around a little when conditions are like this, so you'll more likely encounter him. Deer will lie down for a while, get up, move around, then lie back down. This is done repeatedly throughout the day, so get out among them.

Be sure you have the right clothes for these excursions. If you are comfortable, you'll be successful. Wear soft clothing over the top of waterproof or water-repellent clothing. I can't think of anything worse than being wet and cold and trying to hunt at the same time. Then too, there is always the chance of getting pneumonia, sore back, and all those other goodies!

Most of the guys I know quit hunting when the drizzle starts, or stay right in the sack if they wake up and there it is. I do not advocate hunting in the rain. That's carrying it too far. I prefer to rest during the rain and hunt later. I remember, however, a time when I had only one day left to hunt, and as the alarm banged off in the dreary hours, you could hear the rain spattering on the cabin windows. After muttering to myself, I made breakfast. Twenty cups of coffee later it was still raining briskly, with no sign of letup. I thought of the long wait until next year and galvanized into action. I made sure I was waterproof, then off I went amidst the jeers of the saner members of my party. In half an hour my wool shirt and pants weighed a ton, and sagged down more with every step. My ears were dripping and getting colder by the minute. I knew it would take at least an hour to clean up my rifle. But underneath I was basically warm and dry because of the waterproof rain gear under the wool. I knew where a grove of fair-sized hemlocks stood, and this is where I headed. Just inside the big trees I stopped to take stock. It was nice here! The rain was concentrated off the ends of the branches, and very little of it was penetrating to where I stood. I pressed all the water I could out of the wool shirt and pants, and felt 10 pounds lighter.

I was almost two thirds of the way through the hemlocks when I saw movement ahead. I froze to the trunk of a big hemlock and waited. In a minute I spotted a dandy little buck walking toward me. He stopped and shook vigorously, like a dog. The water flew in a round spray out of his hollow-haired coat. He had his nose to the ground when I raised my rifle very slowly. Just before the trigger squeeze he saw me. I swear his eyes got big, and he seemed to be saying, 'I've got to be out in this, but what are you doing here?' The point is that a really serious deer hunter, pressed to the wall, will do almost anything to get his buck.

I like to hunt in a drizzle, but you ought to see me when there is a gentle, picture book kind of snow! I get positively ecstatic. I'm worse than a kid in a cookie factory. This is the prettiest weather to hunt in I can think of, and the most productive for the still-hunter, alone or with a friend who is adept at still-hunting. The first snows of the year will find deer moving all day, enjoying it as much as humans. Be alert with all your senses. This is not the time to track deer, even if there is enough snow on the ground. As long as you are in the territory where the deer are, move the same as you would without snow, and stay alert. Deer are just as likely to move into you as you are to move into them. I know it is difficult not to pick up prints and try to track the animal down, but stay away from the temptation in this kind of weather. You'll do better just moving through the covert. By this kind of weather I mean a day that is almost windless (winds of 10 m.p.h. or slower), with big, fluffy flakes of snow, sort of like parachuters looking for a place to land.

A radio in camp comes in handy to try to catch the forecasts; if there is none to be had, take a small barometer along. In the event of a storm forecast, or a rapidly falling barometer, you'll know what to do. In the event of a big snowstorm the deer will head for the thickest cedar swamp, or the thickest evergreen stands around. Deer do not like to subject themselves to punishment, so they head for the spot where the wind and snow will be somewhat tamed.

Just before a storm is an ideal time to be out looking. The deer will be active. Old Buck will feed heavily, then move to the sheltered area. He has a built-in barometer to tell him when it is urgent to fill the tank. Watch the barometer, or listen to the forecast, or both; you can be on deck for the action. I hate to hunt in a big storm, so I'll sit it out in the comfort of a manmade contrivance of some type.

After the storm, when the barometer is on the rise and the sky clears, the deer will come out of hiding, frolic and gambol like a bunch of youngsters on a picnic. This is the time to be there with them.

Actual tracking of deer in the snow is a tough business. The buck is well aware he is leaving a trail that anything with eyes can follow. He is more cautious than ever, and watches his back trail constantly; after all, this is where the danger comes from!

I have had hunters who tracked deer in the snow all day tell me they knew they were close to the deer, but couldn't quite see him. How true! Old Buck had them just where he wanted them, right on his backtrail where he could hear them and watch them all the time! A deer will play hide-and-seek with you all day. I believe they almost enjoy this game. When they are ready to stop the game they will take off and join others; deer know about safety in numbers at a time like this.

A good tracker must work at it! You must not only be able to see, but you must be able to distinguish. Anyone could track a single deer in an area. *His* would be the only track. It is very confusing to have your deer join with several others and not leave his name on his track.

The only possible time you should stick on a track like glue is when you have a wounded deer, or possibly when you are working with a partner.

Check the track when you can, but try to determine where the deer is going and intercept him. For instance, if the trail goes over a ridge, go around the point; you may run into Old Buck watching his back trail.

Tracking in the snow is ideal for two men. One takes the track, the other stays back a little and off to the side. The deer will concentrate on the tracker and sooner or later expose himself to the second man. This generally happens on one of the deer's little "checking" circles.

You can't be haphazard if you want to be a buck hunter. Get some kind of a signal game going so you know where your partner is. You'll have to check occasionally

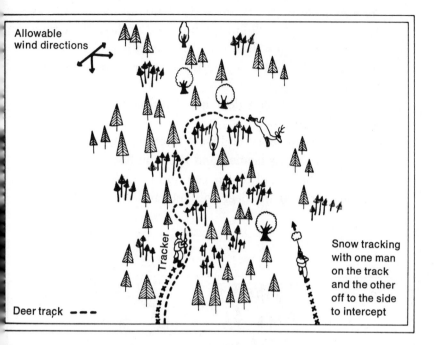

Allowable wind directions

Deer track – – –

Tracker

Snow tracking with one man on the track and the other off to the side to intercept

so you aren't confused. Remember the safety factor, also. You don't want to shoot in the direction of your partner. A birdlike whistle works fine for us. Be sure to have the sounds figured out so you're not led astray by a bird. Do not use your voice, ever!

When a deer is started by one man it generally becomes very occupied with him. This can lead to some interesting times for hunter number two. I know of two men who go through the woods single file. These fellows are very successful because they know their game. The second man stays about 50 to 70 yards back of the first, depending somewhat on the country. They do not move quite as slowly as a single still-hunter, but they do take their time and they stop often. Bob says, "The idea is not to cover a lot of territory, but to cover the territory like a vacuum cleaner."

Don't try to push a deer hard; you can't outwalk him anyway. Move slowly.

When you are alone and want to track, try to figure out where your deer is headed and keep circling to the track. I know it's been said that if you find a track and keep on it, sooner or later the deer will get careless and you'll get

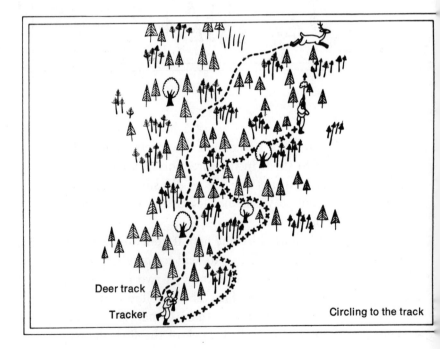

Deer track

Tracker

Circling to the track

him. This may work for cougars and wolves, but it has never worked for me. I guess I get more careless than the deer, or something. Not only that, but in good deer country it would take me a month of Sundays to figure out if I was on the same track! I tried this all day tracking a few times, and I'm sure I tracked a different deer every hour or so. These deer think nothing of walking in each other's tracks.

A couple of years ago Jake was trailing Bob by about 60 yards when he saw a nice buck get up about 40 yards to Bob's right and 15 yards behind. Jake stopped immediately and watched as the buck started to sneak away from Bob. This old whitetail kept his head down and his eyes glued on Bob. He was so intent on watching the moving man that he set a collision course with Jake. Jake was so engrossed in the deer's behavior that he let him get to within 15 feet before he realized it could be a problem to kill this deer. He was *too* close! The buck solved all by putting his nose to the ground on Bob's track. Jake just pointed his rifle at the deer's rib cage and pulled the trigger.

These fellows score better than 50 percent average every year. Some years they both fill, some years only one, but they hunt bucks only, and being human they make mistakes, too. In view of the fact that whitetail hunters throughout the states generally fall in the 12 to 25 percent success ratio bracket (this also includes any-sex season), I'd say they got a good system going! The ability of two men to hunt together as a team, game knowledge, perseverance, and above all patience, really put the racks on the wall.

Whitetails are thought of as creatures that run from

everything in order to escape. This is a bunch of malarky, especially with good-sized or mature bucks. Think about it: if deer did nothing but run when men were hunting them, they would all be dead! You can't shoot them until you see them, so those deer that disappear from view, and stay disappeared, survive. It's as simple as that. Big bucks know they are difficult, if not impossible, to see when they lie down and stay there.

What's the first thing you think of when you want to avoid being seen in the woods? Lying or crouching down, of course. When you played hide-and-seek as a child you instinctively knew you were harder to find if you lie flat on the ground. The armed forces spend scads of time teaching their men the value of getting flat to avoid detection. The lioness trying to make a kill stays as flat as a pancake. Man surely has no corner on the market. Animals, I'm sure, showed us how. Even a giraffe is hard to see when he lies down and puts his head to the ground. He just doesn't look like a giraffe should. This is why you should train yourself to look for parts of a deer rather than a whole animal standing on a golf course.

A buck will think nothing of letting you go by at 15 to 20 feet. As a matter of fact, if the buck hasn't sneaked out long before, he will be inclined to brazen the situation out to the very end.

I almost collected a grizzled oldtimer this way while hunting with six other guys. We were walking together to drive a little basin about a half mile from camp. It was a fairly noisy group at this point, as it was very crisp and frosty. We were walking single file, with me as the last man. While proceeding through a thick conifer area, I saw a branch coming off the shoulder of the man ahead. I ducked and turned my head to the side to avoid a stinging slap in the face. I could hardly believe my eyes! Twenty feet off the path I saw a big buck lying with his chin on the ground! I'd like to say that I swung around and took him on the first jump, but I wasn't even thinking of deer shooting at the time, and for safety's sake I hadn't even loaded my rifle. He took off immediately when he realized the jig was up, and nobody had a chance at him. I even had a helluva time convincing the other guys they had walked by a huge old buck without knowing he was there!

While bowhunting, I crawled up a fallen tree to get where I could see well and rest a while. Shortly, my attention was grabbed by a movement off to my left. A dandy, symmetrically horned buck was coming toward me. At about 60 yards away, while I was thinking how to get into position, he stopped, looked off to his left for a moment, then turned around twice, much like a dog making his bed, and lay down. Once he was down I couldn't see him anymore, but I knew he was unaware of me so I figured to wait him out and see what developed. In about ten minutes a bow hunter appeared, all nicely done up in a camouflage suit. He was moving slowly but steadily on a path parallel to the one the buck had come up on. I wished now for a movie camera to record the action that was about to unfold. Instead I turned around slightly to be ready for instant action myself. It appeared that the hunter would come within 30 feet of the buck. I chuckled a little to myself, wondering how the hunter would handle the situation coming up. But nothing happened. That old buck just stayed right there and let the bow hunter go right on by as if he didn't exist. When the hunter got almost up to my tree he spotted me.

"Ain't no deer around here at all, are there?" he said.

For a fleeting instant I thought of taking him back and jumping that buck, but when I looked over where the buck had been I was just in time to see the rear end of him sneaking out of there.

On another occasion I was witness to an almost unbelievable action by a mature buck. I was resting just off the point of a big ridge when I spotted a buck working his way along about halfway up on the side of the next ridge. The deer was moving almost directly toward my hunting partner, who was still-hunting that same ridge. My partner, Herb, is a good still-hunter, so I decided to watch him in action. The deer stopped, looked back with cocked ears over his shoulder, then turned his head forward and swiveled his ears until they finally locked forward. Then he looked back over his shoulder again. The buck then sneaked about 30 feet farther up the hill, turned around once, and lay down. In a minute I saw the fire-orange of Herb's jacket moving slowly toward the deer. My attention was caught now by another hunter approaching from the direction the deer had come from. That's why he'd been looking back. It was a bad situation. Both hunters were coming on the deer from opposite directions.

If he jumped between them, it could be dangerous. I was about to do something when the strange hunter stopped and sat down. I knew now that when Herb jumped the deer it would go uphill, and breathed a little sigh of relief. Pretty soon Herb was within 25 to 30 feet from the buck and still nothing happened. Herb spotted the other hunter then and stopped. He saw me when he turned around. I pointed vigorously toward the deer. Herb misunderstood my pointing, shook his head affirmatively, then started to come toward me. I did some more vigorous pointing, and all I got back were some waves indicating he knew there was another hunter there. I didn't want to shout "buck" because of the other hunter so I sat back down and waited, resignedly. I wouldn't risk shooting over the head of my hunting partner.

When Herb got within talking distance I told him how close he'd been to a buck, and to step out of the way so I could shoot the deer as long as he didn't want to. He laughed at me and wouldn't budge. I couldn't really shoot anyway, because although I knew where the deer was, I couldn't make out his body clearly. Then the other hunter got up and started to walk up the ridge again.

"Watch!" I hissed.

Herb turned around just in time to see the deer get up and disappear immediately behind some evergreens. Herb's only comment was, "Well, I'll be damned!"

It makes me wonder how many deer I walk by every year, even though I'm aware of their "tricks."

Another still-hunting approach is the casual, steady move. Sometimes this will work in crunchy or dry, noisy weather when it is impossible to be cautious. I have had some measure of success this way, but it is difficult shooting, and you might walk for days and not see a thing. The first time this worked for me was quite accidental. There were about 3 inches of snow, with the top half inch a heavy crust. I swear you could hear a man walk a half mile away. I tried still hunting for a couple of hours, but all I saw was one tail. I tried a drive for my companion, Josh, but you couldn't get to a stand undetected, either. I told Josh I wanted to check the edge of a beech ridge to see whether the deer were using it. As long as the hunting was lousy I wanted to look for a spot for the near future.

Walking in a steady but fairly slow gait, there was nothing about my travel that suggested furtiveness. I was surprised when I saw a doe take two jumps, then look at me for ten seconds. I could have killed her easily. Halfway around the beech ridge I heard a noise, looked around in time to see a nice eight-pointer loping off. This time a lot of luck and the Grace of God were on my side, because my bullet went true. When all else fails and there's nothing else to do, try this. At least you'll be hunting, and when you're hunting there's always a chance.

While still-hunting you run into the strangest situations of any kind of hunting. Once I was hunting an area in northern Wisconsin. Our party hadn't connected yet, and this was the fifth day of the season. My patience was almost exhausted, because the buck pole was still empty and I was as nervous as a minnow in a lake full of bass! I decided to get off alone a couple miles from camp. Alone I could practice all my ideas of hunting without interference from the rest of the gang. Leaving early and traveling swiftly over three hardwood ridges, I planned to hunt a grassy black-brush area. Any bucks in the country should be holed up in this almost impenetrable stuff. The wind was right, so I began to hunt. No one ever hunted as carefully as I did that morning. Everything I did was perfect. I slithered through the thick brush like fog writhing off the creek. Sign showed evidence of deer using the area. In an hour I counted three buck rubs and one old scrape. The territory looked very promising. Another half an hour crawled by with no action. When it did come, it would be close, fast, and furious, but I was confident I could handle it. Then, in the middle of a step, I saw it. There was the unmistakable fork of a deer antler 15 feet away. My heart jumped in my chest. After thirty seconds of balancing on one leg I decided to put the other foot down before I fell over and blew it all. With the foot safely down I had a peculiar feeling that something wasn't right. That buck should have come out of there long ago.

I stood like a statue waiting for something to happen. No matter which way this buck went I'd nail him before he could get 5 feet. Fully two minutes went by. I made up my mind; I'd take another step, because I was in the driver's seat. I finished the step and could see the buck's head. He was facing directly away from me. His rump was only about 6 feet from mine. He had a nice, wide symmetrical six-point rack. His ears laid flat along his thick neck. Just as I thought; somebody had wounded him and he had crawled in here and died. What a shame to lose a nice deer like this. Oh well, I thought, I can't do anything about it. The coyotes and foxes will clean him up.

I relaxed, took my rifle in my right hand, leaned over and poked the buck in the rump. The whole danged marsh came unglued! The rifle went spinning out of my hand as the deer exploded out of there. A Swiss avalanche would have been quiet and slow by comparison! Twenty-six flying bats could have roosted in my gaping mouth. My heart was jumping so wildly nothing short of a fifty-gallon drum could have held it. And if you think this was bad, wait a bit. I heard another noise to my left and looked around right into the gray face of an old whitetail with a huge, wide rack. Where he came from I'll never know. I looked down for my rifle. That big old buck snorted like a bursting steampipe, then he too was gone!

My legs were so rubbery I had to sit down. There were

a couple of deer hairs hanging on the front sight of my rifle and I made myself a deal. If my rifle would never tell anyone about this, I sure wouldn't! And until now it's been my *sole* secret.

Every time I think I have all the answers as far as whitetail hunting is concerned, I get the shaft! Don't try to outguess a whitetail, try to confuse him. If I can de-humanize myself for a short period of time each year, my success with whitetails soars enormously.

I must remember to move slowly and intermittently; look more than I move; not swing my arms or jerk my head; wear good boots and soft clothing; know my weapon intimately; be comfortable; practice diligently all I know about hunting deer; use the weather to my advantage; keep a positive attitude, and never forget that I am the predator and the deer is my quarry.

You can't think like a deer any more than a deer can think like you, so why try?

7. Scrape-Hunting

Scrape-hunting is the least known of all the methods of whitetail hunting, but the most productive when you know the score and apply it. One of the bigest chinks in that armor we have been talking about is the sex urge. After the buck's horns are hard he spends a lot of his valuable time hooking brush and generally polishing his proud adornments. The buck has been without his hard horns for about six months anyway, so now he feels very proud and buckish. The does no longer browbeat him. The fawns give him all their respect, even though he wouldn't think of hurting them. The buck is not quite as secretive as he was all summer, but he is by no means dim or foolhardy, just feeling more like a male animal. About a month after the antlers are hard the buck's neck begins to swell. This is the forerunner of the actual rut, or breeding season.

Weather seems to control the rut to a great degree, but actually it is a combination of both the temperature and the light factor, or the decline of daylight. Were there no freezing temperatures or frost the rut would go on anyway. With no rut there would be times when the whitetail deer would have a fawnless year, and I'm sure you will agree this is not nature's way. In the range of the whitetail the rut generally starts some time in October and continues through December.

When the buck feels the urge coming on he paws out a spot about a foot in diameter. All the leaves, and most of the grass is cleaned down to the bare earth. The buck then urinates onto the spot and paws it around, mixing the materials thoroughly. This is the doe-trap. When the doe comes into her heat period she comes to the scrape to see if the buck is actively using it. She hangs around a while waiting for action. If the buck doesn't show after a time, she urinates in the scrape, then proceeds to the next scrape to repeat. If the scrape is very active, she won't have long to wait. When the buck appears on the scene the doe will be very coy, making a short run or two, inviting the buck to follow. Like most females she only runs fast enough to entice the buck. If it appears that he is falling too far behind, she will slow up enough for him to catch up. The doe remains in heat for three days. If not bred in that time, she will be back in oestrus, or heat, in another month. The buck will generally stay with her until she is bred; sometimes he remains with her the entire three days before he'll look for another doe.

As the season wears on, the buck makes his scrape larger. He often expands his territory, making two or three scrapes. He will travel for some distance to make and check them all. If a scrape is attracting a lot of attention, it will take most of his time to take care of the business at hand. If there aren't very many does in the area, he will abandon the scrape and go to another base of operations to set up shop. A sudden sharp freeze or hard frost seems to trigger an unusual amount of sexual activity in the whitetail world. Sudden changes in the weather, from cold to warm, or stormy, put a temporary hold on the activity. Slow sex activity begins when the weather is mild for any prolonged length of time.

Bucks are quite secretive about where they set up shop. This is why the run-of-the-mill hunter fails to locate the scrapes. Most of the time they are made in the thick country rather than the open. I have seen scrapes along fence lines and at the edge of a clearing, but this is definitely the exception rather than the rule.

The rut, or mating season, does strange things to old whitetail's behavior. There are times when a buck gets positively foolish and doesn't think of anything but sex. Again this is not the general rule, but it does happen. Bucks do not often place anything above their love for life, but this period in their life leaves them a little more vulnerable than usual. It is this urge that causes the deer to move more at night, too. When the car kill goes up dramatically you can bet the rut is in full swing.

When you see a buck traveling along with his nose to the ground and his tail straight out back, he's trailing a doe. This is the time the buck can get so excited he will hop stiff legged, hooking at the brush and grunting at every hop. His eyes will become glassy and often he will stand with his hindquarters sagging. The buck's odor becomes very strong at this time. A trained human nose will pick it up at quite a distance. I have smelled them at close to a hundred yards away when I was downwind. The strong odor comes from the buck's metatarsal glands and from his wallowing in his scrape. Occasionally a buck will become so excited he will rub his shoulders in the mud of the scrape until they are well coated. It doesn't take too much of this before the old boy smells worse than the elephant pit at the zoo! This is also the time when the bucks get into their pushing matches. The whitetail buck does not like competition, so when a strange buck invades his territory he makes no bones about his displeasure. Most of the time the battles are little more than mild pushing matches, but occasionally tempers flare more than usual and the matches become more serious. Once in a great while, especially if the bucks are mature, they will come together with such force as to have their horns become locked together permanently. If they are found in this condition and you are possessed of the idea to separate them, do not be surprised if they turn on you the minute they are free!

So-called tame bucks are at their most dangerous time when they are in the rut. A confined buck will think nothing of charging you on the spot. There is hardly anything you can do to avoid him if he is prone to hook you. Several men have been killed by "tame" bucks in the rut.

Look for scrapes in the vicinity of the buck rubs, and along the buck trails. When you discover a scrape don't go any closer than you have to in order to identify it. The further you stay away from the scrape the better your chances for success when you hunt it. You must be sure a buck is using the scrape, or you will be wasting your time. Try to locate more than one scrape. Approach is the key to success in scrape-hunting. Having several scrapes to hunt enables you to take advantage of the wind and other factors of weather on a given day. If you can't approach a scrape properly, don't approach it at all. Scare a buck at his scrape and chances are you will not see him at that location again for at least two or three days. Your approach must always be upwind. The buck will lie downwind from his scrape so as to wind any doe that might show up. In the event he doesn't actually lie downwind he will always check the location from that direction. You can see the importance of being on the right side of the track! The buck will check the scrape several times during the day to see if there have been any callers. With several scrapes to check he can be a busy guy.

This, then, is the time you can expect to see bucks moving during the day.

I have had bucks appear within minutes after gaining my stand. With a good approach you can expect action at any time of the day. Most of the movement is in the early hours, but there is enough travel during the day to make scrape-hunting very interesting, Whitetails hunted very hard will tend to diminish their breeding activity, especially during the daylight hours. But they do not cool it entirely; they merely find another more secluded spot. The dark of the moon finds the buck more active than ever during the day. The more mature the buck, the fiercer the flame of passion burns. Very young bucks do not service many does when there are mature bucks in the vicinity.

The hardest part of scrape-hunting is getting there. The approach is most difficult. If you think it's mean getting to an interception stand without alarming the deer, wait until you try scrape-hunting! Your chances are about one in four that the buck is in the vicinity checking the scrape. To further complicate matters, your chances of running into a doe near the scrape site are at least three times as good. The point I'm getting at is that active scrapes are lousy with some kind of deer. Even the fawns and year-lings congregate in the vicinity. Maybe this is the deer's way of learning about the birds and bees.

I like to hunt the scrapes alone. That way I have no one to complain to but myself when I mess it up. Like the time I was making the perfect approach to a really hot scrape. The slight breeze was almost directly in my face. I had allowed plenty of time for the approach so there was no hurry. A drizzly rain the night before had dampened the leaves enough so I didn't sound like a tank. I was so confident I would get a buck that I felt in my pocket to make sure I had a plastic bag along for the heart and liver!

My wool pants and shirt made vague woods noises as I wormed through the brush. I reached my preselected stand and mentally congratulated myself on my super prowess at being there without spooking anything. After I was comfortably settled and ready to shoot in any direc-tion I popped an anise flavored hard candy into my mouth so I wouldn't get a dry throat. I knew if I had to clear my throat I was finished. Five minutes went by. Like a spook, a doe appeared switching her tail. She looked back, shook herself a little, then made a fast 20-yard dash! I knew the big buck was about to appear at any second. I swallowed nervously and wished my heart would shut up. I started to swallow again when it happened. I strangled on my own saliva! I went into a paroxysm of violent coughing that brought buckets of water into my eyes, and a burning fire in my throat and chest. As I stumbled to my feet gasping desperately for a breath of air that would save my life, I saw the biggest rack of horns I have ever seen, and probably ever will see, floating out of the picture! I threw up twice, then stemmed the water flow with my red kerchief. I had really blown it! That buck was spooked so bad I never did see him again.

Even if your intentions are good and your approach apparently perfect, you are bound to bump deer out ahead of you occasionally. If you do, and are aware of it, just keep moving on through without hesitating. Pretend you do not have any intentions of stopping. The deer will read this in your intention and merely move out of the way until he's sure you are gone.

A few years ago I was trying to get to my spot to watch a good scrape. It was early morning and a mite crisp. I still had at least 50 yards to go when I heard a deer leave. I figured it was the buck, so I veered off to the side, making enough noise so he wouldn't have to go too far to know I was just stumbling through his area accidentally. I tried to approach the scrape again about noon, but a vagrant eddy of wind gave me away. This time I had a glimpse of his horns for a split second. I made more noise than usual and veered off again. I cracked brush for a quarter of a mile, knowing I hadn't spooked the buck, but curious to see if I had disturbed him enough to cause him to leave his hot scrape for a day or two. That afternoon I tried my approach again. I was all settled and ready for action when it began. Two does came to the scrape. One squatted at the scrape, milled around a little, then moved off. She came by me at about 20 yards. Five minutes later the buck appeared like a genie. He sniffed at the scrape, then wallowed his shoulder in the moist mud. He came out of there crow-hopping and grunting at every hop. He was close enough for me to see his eyes rolling and his chest heaving with excitement. I think I could have had on a neon sign flashing "HUMAN" and he wouldn't have noticed it! The hair flew when I hit him or I never would have known he was hit. His stride never changed and he was still grunting when he piled head on into a birch.

Scrape-hunting holds a special excitement because you're not guessing there are deer in the area. You know they are there and you know a buck is there, because he's the only one that makes a scrape. A lot of other signs may indicate a deer has been there, but a fresh scrape indicates a buck is in the vicinity.

Does and fawns are very prone to complicate scrape-hunting. Even if the doe is busy enticing old buck the fawns are in the area as spectators. I know it's been said that bucks drive the fawns away in the breeding season, but it's just not true. The fawns may be seen and not heard in the very brief breeding season of the doe (three days or less), but they are not separated. I'm sure if you will think about it you'll know the does and fawns are together well into spring.

Well, it's these little guys that make it tougher on the scrape-hunter. You must be able to outbrazen them, and be a statue if they look at you. One afternoon I made a beautiful approach on a scrape and was really patting myself on the back. After ten minutes went by I very carefully and slowly turned my head to observe. When my head got around to the right, I could hardly believe my eyes. About 15 feet away there was a fawn. I'll never know where he came from. His spots were gone, of course, the parietal knobs on his head were clearly visible, he was so close. His twitching black nose gave me about five seconds before he had complete identification. Then he stomped his right front hoof down smartly and snorted probably his first real warning snort. The covert came alive with jumping deer! I saw the big buck for a split second before he disappeared. I sagged back cursing all fawndom. Those deer were so spooked I could forget about this scrape for at least a week, and the season would be over before that.

Horn rattling is most effective in scrape areas. In my limited experience with horn rattling I have found there has to be a large population of deer in the area before horn rattling does anything more than get you blood blisters on all your fingers and the feeling that you are a complete dummy standing out in the woods clacking horns together. I remember a couple of years ago I was very busily engrossed with rattling horns, scratching in the leaves with them, and scraping one up and down on a cedar tree. I had mentally put myself in an old buck's hooves and was fighting mad. In a short time I saw a hunter approaching me. When he got close enough, but not right by me, he asked, "What in the hell are you doin'?"

"I'm rattling horns to attract a buck. What does it sound like I'm doing?" I asked, a little indignantly.

"It sounds like you're a dim-witted human bangin' horns together to scare everything out of the woods! It's workin', too," he said. "I'm leavin', but if you see some guys comin' through the woods with a net, you'll know I sent 'em!"

With that he walked away, shaking his head. I admit

my confidence was shaken somewhat, but I haven't quit trying. I must admit I have never been able to rattle up a buck in Wisconsin, but I did have the opportunity to see it done in Texas. I spent a day with a horn rattler and saw four bucks come for a look. This fellow was the one who told me the place had to be crawling with deer before rattling worked very well.

While I prefer to hunt the scrapes alone, sometimes conditions warrant a partner or two. We have been successful moving a buck away from a scrape into one of our gang. If a buck is particularly difficult for a single hunter,

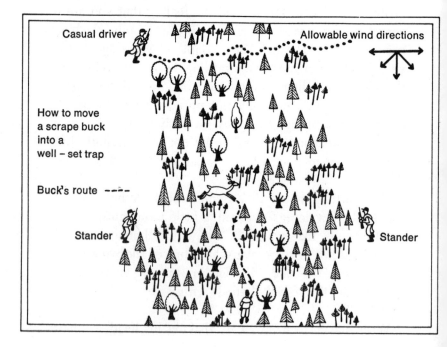

we'll gang up on him a bit. In other words, if a buck makes a dummy of me several times in succession, I get upset.

One of the tricks to remember is the casual drive. Two or three hunters position themselves downwind from the scrape. The object of the driver is to make enough noise and be moving regularly so as to put the buck completely at ease. He'll know all he has to do is to temporarily vacate his territory. The buck will drift downwind easily, then curl off to one side or the other to let you go by. Before he realizes it he's trapped.

You may think this is unfair. I don't! I've had bucks get away from even this seemingly airtight trap more than once.

One of my favorites to pull on a smart, ornery buck is simple. As I said before, whitetails aren't smart. If they were, they'd be able to count. None of the whitetails I know can even count to three or four. Sometimes a buck can't even count to two! Several years ago I enlisted the help of my sons-in-law. There was a particularly hard-to-see buck using an active scrape. I tried for three days to outfox this old boy, but he was too much for me. I planned the attack very thoroughly. The three of us approached the scrape upwind very casually and noisily. I dropped off about 30 yards downwind while the others continued rather noisily on their way. The boys were hardly out of sight when the big, rough, old tenpointer put in his appearance. He shook his horns a few times, looking in the direction of the boys. I almost had a heart pang as the .270 bucked my shoulder, but it was a momentary twinge.

Don't hesitate to gang up on 'em a little. Schemes don't always work this perfectly. The short end of the deal has been dealt me more times than I care to admit!

An experienced scrape-hunter can operate anywhere that whitetails are found. Recently my wife and I had the opportunity to hunt in Saskatchewan. We had never hunted in this particular area before, so we knew nothing of the lay of the land. The time was the second week in November. When we arrived in Redvers we found out there had been a severe winter kill of whitetails, so the deer population was down. After two days of hunting with the affable Canadians, Canadian style, Marg had gathered a beautiful ten-pointer, but I hadn't found a shootable buck. Then genial Ben Gredensky told me of a huge buck that hung out in a 30-acre popple island. So far no one was able to get close enough to do him in, but we would try him in the morning.

Ben drove us out to the area. He was going to position me, and then he and Marg were going to try to move the big boy to me. We just got out of the car when Marg said, "There he goes!" The whitetail was at least 600 yards away, but all I could see was horns! Ben said, "I told you he was a sly one."

We decided to look at the area he came out of. Shortly after we entered the 30-acre spot Marg called for me to come and look. She had stumbled into the biggest love nest I've ever seen. There were three well-used scrapes within a hundred yards, and there were rubs all over the place. Some of the rubbed popples were 8 inches in diameter! I asked Ben if he could come back in the afternoon and pick us up. He said we were daft, but he would figure some way to get away from the hotel.

Three popples had been toppled by the wind about 75 yards from the activity. They were wedged together in such a way as to make a kind of seat about 8 feet off the ground.

The wind direction was perfect, so we elected to use the spot. Three hours crept by and I was glad I had enough clothes on, because the wind was raw. It was necessary to shift positions about every half hour, and you always worry then that you'll spook the deer. About one o'clock Marg hissed, "Here he comes!"

My heart jumped, but it was a false alarm. There was a deer all right, but it was a big solitary doe visiting one of the scrapes. She stuck around for a half hour, which made it triply tough. She urinated in one of the scrapes, then wandered off. I eased into another position, wondering whether it was worth the cramps I was getting. I had just settled down when Marg clicked her tongue. I turned my eyes slowly and there he was! This is typical. Big bucks seem to appear magically out of nowhere. He was a scant 80 yards when the crosshair settled on his rib-cage. The huge twelve-pointer collapsed right into the scrape.

Two hours later Big Ben came to pick us up. His eyes got large as he said, "Got the old boy, eh? We been tryin' to get him for a couple of years now, but you States people hunt different than we do. Maybe you'd show me how?"

Using the proper scent goes along with scrape-hunting. A good glandular scent will help you become accepted in the deer woods. With the numbers of deer you are likely to be in contact with near a scrape you must wear a covering scent, or be prepared to be disappointed.

Scrape-hunting requires a great deal of body discipline. Head and hand movements must be kept to an absolute minimum. When you must move something, do it very slowly and deliberately. Quick movements are never missed by a deer. Even a human sees the wing movements of a bird, where he might miss a fox sneaking by. It's very difficult to remain still for more than half an hour at a stretch. If you feel the need for movement, try tensing all the different muscles in your body separately. It not only relieves the boredom and takes away the crampy feelings, it makes you stronger! This is the dynamic tension Charles Atlas prescribed for giant muscles. If you spend as much time in pursuit of whitetails as I do, and practice these muscle tension exercises religiously, you'll not only be a good deer hunter, you'll be the strongest one in the woods!

8. *Tracking*

The most difficult task I can think of is teaching a person the art of tracking by means of the written word. I can tell you what to look for and how to recognize it, but from there on it is up to you. At the risk of making you angry by being repetitious, I'll have to say that practice is the only way. Practice tracking and hunting in the off season. The more time you spend in the field poking around and noticing what your eyes see, the better equipped you'll be when the season is on.

Tracks hardly ever tell you where a deer is standing; they only tell you where he was. I have yet to plod along with my head down tracking like mad and bump into a buck standing in his tracks watching me!

Since the beginning of time, old whitetail's enemies have attacked from the rear. This age-old fact makes it difficult to approach a whitetail directly on its track. Old buck watches his backtrack very closely for just such guys who will be "hot" on his trail. The most they ever see is the good-bye wave of the tail. Generally they only see tracks and beds day after day.

The most difficult part of tracking is determining exactly how fresh the track is. A buck that was in the area yesterday doesn't have to be in the area today. However, if this buck was in the area yesterday, the day before, and the day before that, chances that he'll be there today rise greatly.

Hunting in an area with no fresh sign is like fishing for lake trout in the bathtub; your chances of getting anything are a little tight!

Recognizing fresh sign can be the difference between a good airing and a successful hunt. There are quite a few hunters who swear by the deer-dropping method of determining whether there are deer in the area. One of these experts took me to an area in the late fall. He had told me the area was positively loaded with deer. After a couple of hours of walking around, I hadn't seen a fresh track. I will admit there were deer scats everywhere. My friend enthusiastically pointed them out. We were, in fact, in a wintering area. My friend was viewing the scats from 6 feet up. Closer examination proved they were old. In the morning dew some of them looked shiny and fresh to the unpracticed eye.

When in doubt at all as to whether a track is fresh, do as I have done many, many times in practice. Carry a deer hoof with you. Imprint a track next to the one you are studying, using 25 to 50 pounds of pressure. (You can try this a few times at home on the bath scale till you get the feel.) By comparing the two you will soon learn what to look for. Types of soil, ground cover, moisture conditions, time of the day—all of these factors have a direct bearing on what a track or part of a track will look like. All snow conditions are not alike, either. Crusty or powdery snows are the difficult ones. Some fellas have a tough time determining the direction of a track in deep snow. Remember, a deer puts his leg almost straight down. When he lifts his leg he drags it forward, so the scuffs in the snow are the direction he went. Many times I have come upon hunters backtracking. I guess they wanted to see where the deer had been rather than where he went! Should there be any doubt in your mind, take off your glove, reach down in the track, and explore it with your fingers. As Staazy told me, "Da points point da direction ole buck go."

Don't be embarrassed when you goof! I often do. We are not living in an age where our livelihood depends on our ability to procure meat in the wild. If you become a good tracker, your chances at game will be more than doubled. For many years I thought tracking was a laughing matter because everytime I tracked something I got laughed at!

Tracking before the shot is mainly determining which direction the buck is headed. None of the hunters in my acquaintance have ever tracked a buck and killed it by staying right on the track. You must try to anticipate where he is going and circle to cut him off. A buck watches his backtrack too carefully, especially when there is snow on the ground. Deer know all about snow and how they leave tracks.

Examining tracks closely can let you guess a lot of

things about the size and kind of animals making them. Size and appearance of deer tracks are not reliable for determining whether the animal is a buck or doe. I know it's been said that a true expert can tell you at a glance whether it was a buck or doe. The buck is supposed to have a huge track with rounded toes from traveling after the ladies. Their *hocks* are supposed to touch the ground much of the time because of their great weight and all that sort of bunk. This sounds good on paper, but in the woods it's different. Both sexes are equipped with the same shoes, which make sort of a split-heart-shaped track with rather pointed toes.

Deer are not made with cookie cutters, so they come in various sizes and weights. Some deer have big feet, some have small feet, just like dogs or human beings. Take the case of Big Julia for instance. My wife and I have watched this doe we call Julia for many years. Julia is a large animal, well built, with enormous feet. I suppose on the hoof she weighs 200 pounds, but she leaves a track like a super-record buck of some kind. Julia's track has caused a lot of hearts to pound, and there has been much hunting in her area for a giant "Phantom" buck that just can't be found in the hunting season! A deer, when moving along ordinarilly, puts its left hind foot into the print of the right front foot, and vice versa. This does two things. It causes the deer to single foot, or leave a straight line track, and sometimes the super-imposing is a little off, causing the track to look larger than it really is. Sometimes an injury will make a lot of difference in the track. I knew another fair-sized doe that had been hit by a car, causing injury to her left hind leg. In the two years I knew her she could hardly put any weight on the crippled leg.

This caused a well-splayed, hocks-down track by the other one. If you didn't know it, or study the track a while, you'd think it was one of those real giants.

Some of those bucks with good racks that don't make it big bodywise just don't leave big tracks. In areas of heavy hunting pressure, where the bucks seldom live long enough to become huge, their tracks will be indistinguishable from the does'. In lightly hunted areas, or areas where the hunting is difficult, the bucks live longer. A mature buck is, except in very rare cases, always taller and heavier than a mature doe. His tracks then should be larger, and I have found this to be true in most cases. The point I'm trying to make is that I don't think there is anyone who can look at a deer track and say definitely whether a buck or a doe left it. Rather than guess in this manner, find the buck trails and the solitary tracks. These are better signs.

Use tracks to tell you the current areas the deer are using. I know several areas that do not become popular with deer until the deer have been hunted a day or two. When I see by their fresh tracks they have moved in, I hunt them.

It's true the bucks are inclined to drag their feet in snow. When the snow is not more than two inches deep and the tracks are connected by scuff marks in the snow all the way, you can be fairly sure a buck did it. They shuffle more than does. Does pick up their feet like ladies.

For group hunting, the most common use of tracking before the shot is checking areas to be driven for incoming tracks. If tracks indicate deer in that area now, the drive is planned. After the drive, it is easy to check where the deer traveled and how they escaped. This information is very helpful for the next drive. I use tracks before the shot only as a means to tell me where the deer are traveling, and how often.

Tracks are the only way sometimes to trap those golden-age bucks that have a better knack than James Bond for getting out of tight situations. One huge old fellow I knew hung out occasionally in a steep rock-walled canyon. I saw him go into this place one morning. I rounded up a few friends, placed them on strategic stands, and thought we had him. None of us saw or heard him. He couldn't have gone out the far end without running into opposition. The sides were impossible for him to scale, and even if he did, we'd have seen him. The only way out was a backward sneak. Two days later we went in again. This time I made sure the entrance was well covered. No one saw him! After grumbling at my ineptness and apparent bad eyesight, everyone left. I began to comb the area inch by inch. I was prepared to kill a day of hunting to find out how the old boy was doing it. Several hours later, after really searching, I came on his track headed for the left wall. On the left wall was a fissure, or opening, about 3 feet wide that wasn't visible until you were right on it. This cut wound upward for 50 feet or so, then cut back on a little bench which was covered by a thick growth of cedars. From there it was easy going up the path and over the rim. The next day I couldn't convince the skeptics that I knew how the old boy escaped. My wife believed me, though, and I placed her just back of the rim so he'd come right into her. I figured if the old boy was there, he wouldn't bother with any other way out as long as this had worked so well, so the two of us would be able to work him. Half an hour later I heard the dull "poonf" of Marg's .270 behind the rim. The buck had come through as though he were on a railroad track. She shot him at 50 feet, and you should have seen the skeptics when we got back! I don't believe this buck would have used this canyon at all if there had been snow on the ground.

In dryland tracking remember that deer don't always leave perfectly indented tracks all over; the terrain doesn't permit it. Some ground is hard, some rocky, some grassy, some so covered with leaves or pine needles that it's very difficult to find tracks. Patience is required. I remember one rocky area the deer were using. It looked impossible to find a track anywhere until I noticed moss and lichens growing on the rocks. By looking at all angles I was able to define a deer runway by the way the moss and lichens were worn off the stone.

In sandy country it is easy to find tracks, but difficult to tell how fresh they are. To be sure deer are using the runway take a branch and brush out all the tracks for 20 feet or so. Then check it next day. A similar method is being used by conservation department personnel in quite a few states. In the sand country, trucks dragging chains or various other articles designed to wipe out all previous tracks are dragged on the backroads in the afternoon. The next morning the tracks are noted just before the roads are dragged again. Several days of this in an area gives them a fairly accurate record.

In dry country it is difficult to tell how old the tracks are. I do a lot of guessing in arid places just like everyone else. Another thing about dry areas is the lack of dew or frost, even making early morning tracking difficult.

After the shot, tracking ranks very high in the order of what to know to have that little edge over other hunters. In order to be a humane hunter you must know how to recover the deer once you have shot it. Countless deer go to waste every year because of ineptness on the part of the hunter. The number one thing I learned early in life was to mark the spot well where the animal was when you fired at him, and which way he went. Pick out some feature to identify with—a windfall, a stump, a particular tree or bush. *Don't guess!*

The first deer I ever shot at kept going after the third shot. I went over to look where he was traveling, but when I got there I couldn't find anything. I was looking half-heartedly when my partner arrived on the scene. I told him I shot at a nice buck, but guessed I didn't hit him, because there was no hair or blood. We decided to hunt some more so my partner started walking away. He had gone about 25 yards when he said, "Somebody must have poked one here, there's a chunk of hair and a bunch of blood." I walked over quickly. There was no snow, but the hit showed clearly. It was a simple matter to follow the big blood trail for about 60 yards. There he lay! My first eight-pointer. If my partner hadn't chanced on the blood trail I never would have found that deer. It is very easy to misjudge the spot unless you select a reference. If you do not find the track immediately when you reach the spot, hang your cap there so you don't get to wandering without having a spot to refer to.

You may even want to hang your jacket in the brush and go back to the place you shot from in order to re-check your directions. Don't assume anything; always check it out. A lot of deer don't act as if they have been hit, when in fact they have been mortally wounded. Any deer that you've shot at should be thoroughly investigated. Just because it didn't fall in its tracks doesn't mean it isn't going to shortly. Sometimes it's very evident you have a hit. The buck may stagger or thresh around in an aimless manner. A deer hit too far back will generally hump up for a jump or two. A chest-shot deer will sort of crow-hop rather than bound normally. A liver-shot deer will not give evidence of being shot. You can usually see when a leg is broken.

Finding the track but no blood or hair right away means you ought to follow it at least 30 to 40 yards. A deer hit fairly high in the chest may not throw any blood that's easy to find until he goes down. The blood has to fill the chest cavity first. The bullet should clip some of the brittle hair off, but if the bullet enters angling from the rear it may not clip a single hair. The color of the hair will give you an idea where the deer was hit. White hair is found on the throat, belly, and rear end. Short brownish hair is found on the legs, black-brown hair on the brisket, grayish-brown hair on the rest of the body. The higher on the body the hair grows, the coarser it is.

There is a great difference of opinion on whether to sit down and wait fifteen minutes to a half hour before pursuing wounded game or whether to pursue immediately. My advice is to pursue and push immediately! Don't wait around for a deer to lie down and stiffen up. Pure bunk!

Take advantage of all the shock your bullet has caused. When a deer recovers from his initial shock he may give you a long run. A lot has been said about a wounded deer lying down and bleeding to death. A deer is a tallowy animal whose body has a strong inclination to plug any leaks it may develop if given the time. A bullet does not cut flesh, it crushes and mutilates it. By smashing tissue it gives the blood vessels a chance to close off; the blood coagulates and tissue repair starts immediately. A razor cut bleeds freely and profusely, a smashed finger does not. Tallow tends to close the entrance and exit holes of the bullet if the deer is quiet. You know very well that if *you* were wounded, the first instructions would be to lie down and become immobilized. Why? So there won't be an extra load on the heart causing it to beat harder and faster. The more action of the body the more it bleeds. I had never heard of a medic saying, "Walk out, soldier, the exercise will make you feel better!" The first-aid book says, "Stop the bleeding, then treat for shock."

Allowing a deer to rest enables it to recover at least somewhat from the initial shock and have a greater determination to get away from its pursuer. A rest may help the body to recover its blood pressure and the animal will regain its strength greatly. Even a gut-shot deer will become very sick right after the shot, but the sickness disappears with rest, and even though death is inevitable, the deer will travel a long way. It is a lot easier to approach a sick deer than one that is only concerned with eluding a pursuer. If there is no snow, the deer that stops bleeding is almost impossible to find. It's hard enough to follow a wounded animal, even if it continues to bleed. If you can, keep 'em bleeding! A deer has a tremendous vitality and tenacity for life, but a body that keeps losing blood gets weaker every step. Ask any doctor.

Try to determine, from the hair and blood you find, where the deer was hit. Light-red blood indicates an artery was severed; your tracking should be easy and recovery quick. A little froth with the light-red blood indicates a lung shot. Again a quick recovery is indicated, especially when some of the blood is directly on the trail.

This indicates bleeding from the nose or mouth. Dark-red blood means the deer is hit somewhere else besides the "boiler room," with the exception of heart shots. I have seen heart-shot deer run a hundred yards before collapsing. A deer with a broken front leg will run you dizzy; your chances of catching up are slim. but a deer with a broken hind leg should be recovered. It is difficult for a deer to travel with a broken hind leg as their hind legs are the primary propelling force, and without the full use they become exhausted quickly. On the other hand, I have taken a couple of deer that were three legged, with a front leg gone. The legs were well healed, and the deer experienced no particular difficulty traveling.

A difficult deer to track was a magnificent buck my wife Marg shot. The 130-grain .270 smashed the stifle on his right rear leg and splattered some fragments into his belly wall. He was traversing a steep slope when she fired. At the shot he went down like a load of gravel behind a little bench. I congratulated her and we went down to look. He wasn't there! I looked around and found some rather short brown hair and white hair. Then I saw some bone fragments and blood. Then Marg hollered, "There he goes!" He was on the valley floor and working it rather well at about 400 yards. I glassed him quickly and saw that his right rear leg was broken. Then he was gone. We hurried down to where we had last seen him. The country was sandy and not too heavily wooded; I didn't have any trouble finding the track. The wound was dripping blood in drops the size of a dime. The weather was unseasonably warm and the sand was dry. This, compounded by the multitude of cattle and deer tracks, began to make the tracking job slower.

In another quarter mile the blood trail began to thin down. The drops were getting small and very difficult to find. We had slowed considerably, giving the buck a chance to rest a little and start to wander. I wanted to put more pressure on him so he'd have to move out, but I didn't know how. Then Marg came up with the idea we have used many times since. Every drop of blood we found we tied a piece of red hanky on the grass. When five or six cloths were on the grass I was able to stand back and get the exact line the buck was traveling. It was much easier to find the trail now, and when we had a couple of hundred feet covered this way I had Marg stay at the last blood while I took off on this line. A hundred and fifty yards ahead I came on a better blood trail. We had made the buck move faster, and his leg wound had broken open, leaving a blood trail fairly easy to follow. The easier to follow, the faster we went, and the more blood was on the trail. In less than a half mile Marg spotted the buck lying down, watching his backtrail. She broke his neck with a well-placed shot. Pure tenacity, combined with a desire to kill a wounded animal as quickly and humanely as possible, did the trick in this case. I'm sure the buck would have died before morning, but this way he was converted into a real trophy.

Impatience causes a lot of lost venison every year. It seems incredible that a hunter who has been still for hours waiting for that once-a-year opportunity to bag a deer would refuse to spend more than five minutes looking for evidence the animal has been hit solidly or, once the evidence has been found, take the time to pursue and recover.

I like to see a quick kill, but some of my most thrilling

hunting experiences have been in the pursuit and recovery of wounded game. I suppose I was lucky to have a neighbor like John to teach me patience in tracking. I considered myself a fair tracker until I met John. My wife shot at a big dry doe we knew had been hanging in the area. The doe staggered, lay down for a minute, then lurched over a small knoll out of sight. I arrived at the scene a couple of minutes later, as I was the one who had moved the doe to Marg. We found where Marg had hit the doe. The area was well splattered with blood, in fact for 25 feet or so it looked as though someone had painted the trail with a 6-inch brush. I was confident we would find the deer right over the little oak knoll, but she wasn't there! The blood trail led down into a very thick swamp. After about 200 yards the blood trail petered out. I became very upset at losing the trail. After about ten minutes or so of looking around I told Marg the deer must have recovered. I didn't really believe it and of course Marg was very unhappy. We went back to where Marg had hit the deer. The evidence of a good hit was still there, and so was my neighbor. "Need any help draggin' it out?" John said. I told him what happened. He said he'd help me, because no deer could lose that much blood in such a short distance and make it.

It took quite a while to get back to where I'd lost the trail. John explained to me on the way that I should never walk on the trail myself, because I'd destroy the sign in case I needed to refer back. I could plainly see I had trampled the trail badly. At the end of the line, John sat down and lit a cigarette. I was chomping at the bit to get going, and said so. John told me to calm down and start looking again while Marg stayed at the last blood. I started looking, but my heart wasn't in it. The ground was frozen and there was no snow. Then John said softly, "Here's some blood." I went over to look. The blood spot was about as big as the head on a nail. John told me to stay at the blood spot until he found another. My blood pressure was up quite a ways by the time John found another speck of blood. It was clear now that the deer had gone at a right angle from where I'd lost it. John stayed at the last blood until I found the next blood, which was drop size. We leapfrogged like this for an hour, covering 150 yards or so. Again I got antsy. Then John squared me away. "Do you want this deer or don't you? If I weren't helping you with this one I'd be hunting my own!" All of a sudden it occurred to me that John wasn't a doddering oldtimer, but a very sharp-eyed, painstaking, adept craftsman, and I was the dummy! Almost immediately I began to contribute to the job. Instead of scanning, I looked searchingly. Then John told me to circle ahead about a hundred yards. In very short order I came upon the doe, unable to rise. I dispatched her quickly. Marg was tickled and so was I. I thanked John for the help verbally, but mentally I really thanked him for the lesson.

Even in snow, when you are tracking an animal, stay off the track yourself. A mortally hit deer may not show any blood, even in good snow, for 60 to 100 feet. If you shoot at an animal, be sure to check it out for at least 100 feet.

My uncle once shot at an eight-pointer that jumped in the heavy black brush he was going through. A single snap shot was all he had, although he saw the tail wave a couple of times after that. When I asked if he got him, he said he hadn't. When we got through the brush I asked him if he'd checked the track. He hadn't. I took him back in the brush and he showed me where he had shot from. We found the buck's bed and track easily. For the first five or six jumps there was no sign of a hit. Uncle said, "See, I told you I didn't hit 'im." Then the next jump indicated where the buck's legs splayed to the side. The next indicated where the buck bounced off a popple. Well, bucks don't often do that! Three jumps later we found him stone dead, half covered with snow! Ben's shot must have caught the animal on the jump, as it entered just behind the last rib and ranged downward through the heart, lodging in the brisket, but not going all the way through. We found one drop of blood in the next to the last jump. Ben now checks every shot carefully.

A few years ago a big whitetail surprised me by being on a small, almost barren hill when I turned around to see where I'd been. I brought the rifle up smoothly, and when the crosshairs looked right on his shoulder I squeezed. He jumped and angled across the hill, then disappeared before I could shoot again. I thought I'd heard the bullet hit, but wasn't too sure. When I got there I couldn't find a thing. The hill was rocky and hard. There were a few shoulder-high patches of oak brush scattered here and there. I looked for twenty minutes without finding a single clue—no hair, no blood, no track. Then I stood exactly where the deer had been. I had marked the spot by a single clump of waist-high brush. I estimated the angle of his travel and scoured the area. Nothing. Then I started again, but this time directly across the hill. I knew he hadn't gone this way, but tried it as a last resort. About 15 or 20 feet away I came on a single print in a small depression. It pointed straight ahead. Ten minutes later I found the big boy piled up under the oak brush. I had mistaken his line of travel, partly because he was 230 yards away and I was looking into the late afternoon sun. The shot had taken him right in the shoulder and ranged slightly back into the lungs. I don't know why, but there was no hair or blood anywhere.

I have found it is the small clues that really pay off, like a small deviation in stride after you have shot, or the sound of the bullet hitting at the longer ranges. A deer that rears up is generally hit, one that kicks out behind with both feet like a horse is hit well. Any hunching or pulling together indicates a hit. Any vocal sound from the deer indicates a hit. A definite quickening of pace by the deer is a good sign for the hunter. The position of the flag or tail means nothing. A well-hit deer may wave his flag as well as a healthy deer.

Look for the small ground signs after a hit—scuffed leaves, broken branches, blood on limbs or trees, splayed tracks, hair on branches and trees.

Your ears can tell you whether an animal is in trouble. Brush crackling, leaves scuffling, heavy, labored breathing; all of these are indications of a hit.

While tracking, make darn sure you don't get so engrossed in the track that you forget to look ahead constantly. Try not to be noisy, so if the animal does move you can hear him. If you have two to do the tracking, and the track is easy, have one do nothing but be alert for the wounded animal. Should the animal go into a heavy thicket, which they often do, two men can spread out and circle him somewhat. Above all, don't give up until all possibilities have been exhausted.

Squirrels often tell me where the wounded deer is, but the best of all tattletales is the blue jay. There is nothing a jay bird likes more to bedevil than a deer, wounded or not. He can often tell you where the deer is when you're ready to give up.

Marg shot at a fork horn with the shotgun. He went down, but got back up and staggered off before she could shoot again. The blood trail was meager, but Marg insisted she had hit him well. The trail led down to the marsh where there was a foot of water. About 50 feet into the marsh I gave up completely; it was impossible to find a trace. Then about 150 yards away a blue jay squawked up a storm. I looked at Marg; she said, "Let's go." When we got fairly close I could see the jay in a medium-sized tree looking down. Fifteen feet closer I made out the head and neck of the deer under a windfall. I was just ready to shoot when his head fell, and that was it. Marg looked up at the jay and said, "Thanks, bigmouth!" The buck was hit a little far back, and high in the chest. Fatal? Yes, but without the jay we would never have found him.

Tracking is a matter of common sense and acute training of your eyes and brain to correlate what's available. The signs and sounds are always there as the ingredients for an enjoyable and successful hunt. All you have to do is mix them in their proper perspective, much like any other recipe, and you will be rewarded proportionately.

9. Care of the Meat

POW!! The buck goes down in a heap, twitching spasmodically. Those powerful hind quarters can be devastating, so stay at a discreet distance until you are sure the deer is dead. Like the oldtimer says, "A deer is never venison until it's dead!" How true, much to the dismay of hundreds of hunters every year.

There are lots of signs to tell you when old *Odocoileus Virginianus* has expired. First, a deer dies with its eyes open, never closed. When you approach your downed deer do it from his back or the rear and be ready to give him another one! If his eyes are closed, don't hesitate; shoot him where it'll do the most good, generally in the neck.

Don't be like Abe Jensen. Abe downed a fine buck. When he got there the deer was flat as yesterday's beer.

Abe leaned his rifle on the deer's horns, noticing the eyes were tightly closed. He got his knife out of its sheath, walked around to the rear of the buck and grabbed the hind leg to turn him over. The next thing Abe knew was when he woke up to find blood all over the place—his! When that deer kicked it drove the butt of the heavy knife right between Abe's eyes, flattening him like a pole-axed steer. Then the blade caromed off his left ear, neatly slicing it all the way through. Although the amount of blood was considerable, Abe thanked his lucky piece the damage was not. The deer was gone, and it only took Abe a quarter hour to find his rifle with the scope smashed. Think what could have happened, and you'll have to agree Abe was lucky.

Now, just because the deer's eyes are open doesn't mean he's dead, either. Rick Stevens can tell you about that. At his shot the buck collapsed. Congratulating himself, Rick approached the deer, noting how lifeless it appeared. The buck's eyes were wide open and staring. Rick turned the buck onto its back. The hind legs fell into a bunched position, just as they should. Rick placed his knife point against the side of the anus and gave a quick jab. Those powerful hind quarters reacted like a medieval catapult! Each rear leg took Rick on his shoulders with matched precision. His 210 pounds was lifted off the ground, and he covered about 5 feet before his back slammed against a tree. His wind completely gone, Rick could only lie there trying to suck in a gasp of air while the buck took off. That buck may still be living, for all we know, and Rick thanked his lucky button he was so close to those hind legs; he could have been killed instead of pushed.

After looking the deer over at a safe distance, make sure

the eyes are open and all signs of breathing have stopped. If you can see the eye glazing, it's a good bet your deer has expired, but don't take a chance. Find a long weed, or cut a long skinny branch and touch the deer's eye in the forward corner. If it blinks, the deer is still alive; if nothing happens, you can rest assured the deer is dead. No matter what state of life the deer is in there will be an involuntary reaction to a foreign object in the eye. You can toss some foreign matter in the deer's eye if it suits you better.

Should the deer still be alive, shoot it. Don't try to knife it to death, or cut its throat. I know a lot of people, including some *big* boys, but I can't think of anyone who can handle a deer, even if it's half dead.

Now that the deer *is* dead, don't bother to cut its throat to bleed it. The minute the heart stops beating, all blood flow ceases except for drainage. So forget "sticking" a deer. I have seen a lot of sorry guys who wanted to have the head mounted but hacked the hell out of the neck trying to "bleed" the deer. Most of the blood will be found in the body cavity.

Once the deer is dead, the sooner you take care of it the better your meat will be.

There is a lot of talk about cutting the metatarsal and tarsal glands off before you do anything else. It is said these glands affect the taste of the meat. Pure bunk! These glands do not affect the meat while the animal is alive; why should they after the animal is dead? Should you be dumb enough to cut these glands off, won't all the gunk be on your knife? Leave the glands alone and you'll have no problems. Keep your hands off them completely.

Be careful when you cut through the belly wall so as not to puncture the intestines. Once through, use two fingers to lift up the belly wall and use your knife between the fingers. Genitals can be removed anytime; they do not affect the flavor of the meat, either. Cut carefully around the anus. You don't want to puncture it or cut into the hams. Some fellows like to carry a short length of string or twine to tie off the anus after it is freed. I like the idea. After the abdominal cavity is open you'll run into the diaphragm, which is a muscular layer separating the lungs and heart from the rest. Go easy and cut this away from the ribs all the way around. Then reach up as far as you can into the neck and sever the windpipe and gullet. Everything should be loose now, so roll it all out of the cavity. Watch out for the bladder. It is located in the canal that takes the large intestine to the anus right on top of the "aitch" bone. If your deer has just gotten up, the bladder will be full. It will feel just like a small bag of water. Be careful not to break the bladder or squeeze the contents out of the tube. Urine and meat are not compatible in my book! Next move the deer a little way and turn it belly down to get all the blood out. I generally carry some paper toweling along to wipe the deer's cavity after it has drained. If you don't have any paper, use grass, which will work fine, but don't use leaves! If any of the intestines have been broken, you must wipe the cavity thoroughly, immediately. Intestinal and stomach fluids taint the meat quickly. DO NOT wash the cavity with water unless you plan to process the deer immediately. Even then I do not approve. Water and meat are not compatible either. The only portions of venison that should see water are the heart and liver. These should be soaked overnight in ice water. Don't pitch them out, because they are delicious.

There is a lot of controversy about how far to open a

1. Start your cuts carefully around the anus.

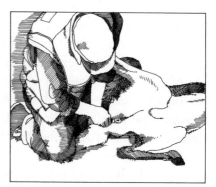

2. Cut carefully around anus.

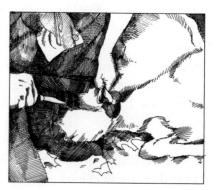

3. Anus completely free; ready to tie off with string.

4. Cut through belly wall carefully, then insert two fingers and lift up so you can cut easily.

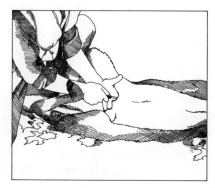

5. Cut carefully up to brisket.

6. Cut genitals out and cut down to aitch bone at hams.

7. Cut the diaphragm carefully
   away from the ribs.

8. Pull diaphragm loose
   from the back.

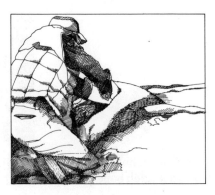

9. Reach way up and cut wind
   pipe and gullet loose.

10. Everything rolled out for a nice clean carcass.

11. Turn over and drain well to get all the blood you can out of the chest cavity.

12. Drain the rear also.

deer to eviscerate it. This depends on all the factors in-volved. The idea is to cool the meat quickly, thoroughly, and keep it clean. If you have a long way to drag the animal through sand, leaves, or other loose material, keep the opening small until you get to camp. Then hang the deer immediately. I much prefer to hang a deer by the hind legs, as you get good drainage out of the best parts of the meat. Nick the veins at the ham and "aitch" bone after you hang the animal. The hams will really drain. Once in camp the deer should be opened wide and propped open with a good circulation of air around it. If the deer is going to have to remain in the field for any length of time, prop it open wide and get it up off the ground, even if you have to just drape it over a log or brushpile. Make sure the animal will be in the shade all day if you can. In case of rain or snow you must protect the cavity by keeping it down.

In those areas where there is a possibility of dust and/or flies be sure to carry cheesecloth bags with you for protec-tion of the carcass. Cheesecloth lets the carcass breathe, but excludes the nasty blowfly and most of the dust. If you are concerned about the weight involved carrying cheesecloth, you aren't strong enough to be hunting. Black pepper is a good fly deterrent. Carry a quarter-pound can with you. Use it liberally after you wipe your deer out and hang it up. Be sure to dust the nose, mouth, and ears. Should you be some distance from camp and notice flies, dust the deer cavity immediately. Wiping the cavity al-ways leaves a thin coating of blood which dries hard and is also a deterrent to flies.

Transporting the carcass from field to home base can present problems. Remember to keep the beast clean and cool; never park your car in the sun while you take a driving break, especially if you have covered the carcass with a canvas or tarp. While traveling on gravel or dusty roads, don't tie the deer onto the rear deck of your car or just throw it in the back of the pickup. You wouldn't think of butchering a beef and letting it lie in the sun, or rolling it around in the sand, or not cleaning it perfectly inside. Well, venison, to be tasty, must be treated the same way you would handle beef.

I do not like to eat fresh venison (except for the heart and liver). It does strange things to my digestive system. I strongly suspect that others are equally affected.

A deer should be hung from one to ten days, depending on the temperature. At 65 to 70 degrees, twenty-four to thirty-six hours is just right. At 50 degrees, three to four days, depending upon humidity, will do, and at 35 to 40 degrees, hang the carcass for seven to ten days, again depending upon humidity. Always let your deer age in the skin if you can, unless it's hung in a controlled-temperature room. The skin is a wonderful insulator and temperature regulator. At deer hunting time the sun is only up about ten hours a day, of which only about five hours are the warm time. Keep the sun off the meat and it will stay much the same temperature as it is at night. I'm not saying it's wrong to skin the animal, cheesecloth it, and hang it, but I much prefer to keep the meat clean and get away from the heavy brown crust that develops on the surface of skinned meat. The skin will also keep moisture off the carcass surface.

The top of the car or wagon is the best place for the deer in dusty country. When you transport one in a pickup, arrange to cover the box so it's dustproof.

Remember to treat and handle the meat just as you would treat a fine hindquarter of beef and you'll have no problems.

I have heard the hue and cry about having absolutely aseptic conditions for the killing and handling of beef. The government must inspect not only the processor, but also the retail stores. The meat must be kept at a certain temperature, etc. I knew of an inspector, George, who was also a deer hunter. He hunted with a garage mechanic who used his pickup for transportation. I happened to be in town one day when they pulled in with a yearling buck thrown in the pickup box. The box was liberally coated with oil, gas, grease, and now blood. Everything had a good coating of sandy dust from the road. I mentioned that size buck should be fine eating.

"I don't care for 'em," George snorted. "I've never had a good one yet. They all got that wild taste."

"George ought to know," his partner said. "He's a meat inspector, you know!"

"How would you stamp that one, with the oil and dust on it, if it came down the line?" I asked. Then I left amid mutterings and face reddenings!

I age my deer by how it smells, but I have been doing it for years and years, and you have to know what you are doing. Good venison like good beef is better a little more aged than too green. Just make sure it is aged and not fresh.

If there is anything I hate, it is hair on or in the meat. By skinning the animal yourself you have only yourself to blame when the meat is hairy. Deer hair is brittle and difficult to control, so take a little more time. If you do sprinkle hair on the meat, get it off. A stiff bristle brush works fine. Tell your processor you don't take kindly to hair on the meat, and maybe you won't have to do as I did many years ago before I processed my own meat. Karl always did a land-office business with deer processing in our small community. When I took my deer there I told him exactly how I wanted it: sliced, not run through the band saw; no hair, no bone meal, no marrow and no tallow spread all over the meat. Even if I had to pay more I would do it gladly, I told him. I got the meat back all wrapped for freezing. I opened a package for supper and almost threw up! There was hair on the meat, and the tallow and bone marrow were ground right into the chops. It took Marg and me and the kids several hours to open the packages and dehair, demarrow and detallow the meat—all but one package of chops. Three months later I invited Karl and his wife over for dinner. You guessed it, Marg served the untreated chops. You could smell them for a country mile! When I passed the chops to Karl, he took the smallest one and began to toy with it. After picking off hair for three minutes and piling it on the side of the plate like hay, he tried a bite. That old bone marrow and tallow almost gagged him! Then Marg brought in another plate of chops. Dehaired, detallowed, and deboned, they were scrumptious. Karl looked at me and said, "Man, you sure know how to bring home your point!"

I process *all* of my own meat now, and have for years, unless I'm caught away from home at a place where it is impossible to do. (I've only had this happen once in the last ten years.) Then I will explain to the processor exactly what I want, even if I have to write it down. Venison tallow and bone gets rancid or icky tasting after a couple of months in the freezer. I bone everything out but the rump roast, which we devour within a month. The other meat is divided into four categories: roasting, frying, stewing, and hamburger or sausage.

Roasting meat (besides the rump) consists of boned, rolled round. Frying meats are the boned loins, both shoulder and backstrap (ordinarily considered the chops) and slices off the round. Stew meats are those portions from the shoulders, rounds, neck, and the lean odd pieces you can cut into ¾-inch-square cubes. These are also very good for stabbing and frying in deep fat at the table. The rest is hamburger or sausage. Now hamburger is *not* junk meat. In order to be the way I like it, hamburger must all be clean, clear, meat. No tallow, no shot areas, no hair, no bone. Depending on how you like it, you add 2 pounds of beef plate to every ten pounds of venison, or 2½ pounds of pork shoulder to every 10 pounds of venison. Either is delicious, but that fixed with the beef plate will be great even if kept in the freezer for a full year! If you like more fat in your 'burger, increase the mixtures by a half pound more of beef plate or pork shoulder. Be sure to have the meat ground, then mixed thoroughly, then ground again.

A sausage enthusiast will take some of the meat to a good sausage maker. I have one sausage maker make metwurst and summer. Another does the knackwurst and ring bologna. Even if you took only enough meat to make 15 pounds of each, you would have a good buck half gone for sausage alone, considering that this poundage is all pure meat.

Brother, if you don't like venison, you don't like meat!

At today's meat prices, a fair buck is worth a minimum of $100. If you point it out, this always helps the old girl to put the seal of approval on deer chasing.

10. Cookbook

Now for the best part. The hunting is such a short time, but the eating can go on all year. I'm not going to tell you venison tastes like beef. I wouldn't want it to! The meat is finer textured, darker in color, and for folks who have to watch their waistlines, it has fewer calories than beef.

Recipes are gathered through the years. Here are some tried and true mouth-watering favorites. Just as with beef recipes, it's impossible to print them all. You can use venison in place of beef in most recipes, remembering your venison is fat free, and you must add some beef fat in those recipes that need it. Because most of your venison is fat free, it does not go well on the charcoal broiler if sliced thin, since it turns out rather dry. The exceptions would be a round roast of 4 pounds or better, or whole loins.

Keep in mind the recipes that really grab you when you freeze your venison. We mark all our packages accordingly—cubed venison, rolled ham for roast, round steak for frying, round steak for Swiss, etc. This enables you at a glance to select the right package for your recipe. Also, it's a good idea to mark your venison as to where you got it, geographically that is.

Different sections of the country cook their venison just as differently as other dishes. These recipes are not only Marg's own favorites, but favorites we have gathered through the years from many different states. I have been fortunate to run across many fine cooks who would prepare their favorite venison dishes for me to sample. It's not always easy to pry the actual recipe from them. Marg has translated the small pinch, large pinch, the smattering, etc. into terms we all understand, bless her heart!

Some of these recipes are taken from mule deer cookers. Mule deer and whitetail recipes are readily interchangeable. The meat is very similar, as is Angus, Hereford, or Holstein steer's meat.

If you like lamb ribs barbecued, you would like venison ribs. Venison hamburger can be used in any dish because of its similarity to beef hamburger.

Most hunters have a taste for a cocktail or two, so while you're cocktailing and spouting off about all those fantastic shots you made, try these hors d'oeuvres.

VENISON LIVER TIDBITS

2 lbs. deer liver, peeled
2 tbsp. salt
1 tbsp. white pepper
2 tbsp. dried marjoram flakes
1 large Spanish onion, diced
½ tbsp. curry powder

¾ cup water
1 can water chestnuts, sliced
   in thirds
1 large can mushrooms
⅓ cup port wine

Cut livers into 1-inch cubes, mix with salt, pepper, marjoram, onion, curry powder, and water. Bake, covered, at 290 degrees for four hours. Add water as needed to keep moist. Five minutes before serving add water chestnuts, mushrooms and wine. Serve hot with toothpicks and tidbit crackers. Makes about 60 pieces.

LIVER PASTE

1 lb. peeled venison liver
   (young deer)
2 hard boiled eggs
1 small onion

Lemon juice
1 tbsp. Worcestershire sauce
Mayonnaise enough to make
   a spreading consistency

Boil liver until tender. Grind very fine. Add liquids and mayonnaise till it is of spreading consistency. Have plenty of cocktails and crackers handy; they'll really go for this!

SOUTHERN WISCONSIN MEATBALLS

2 lbs. finely ground venison
2 lbs. finely ground lean pork
2 tbsp. salt
¾ tsp. white pepper
2 tbsp. dried marjoram flakes
1 medium onion, finely
    ground
1 egg

4 tbsp. bread crumbs
½ tsp. sweet paprika
About 1 gallon water
About 3 tbsp. salt
3 bay leaves
1 large onion studded with
    cloves

Mix venison, pork, 2 tablespoons salt, pepper, marjoram, ground onion, egg, bread crumbs, and paprika. Roll into 1-inch balls. Bring water to a boil, add 3 tablespoons salt, bay leaves, and clove-studded onion. Drop meatballs into boiling water and boil twenty minutes. Drain and serve hot in sauce. Makes about 40 meatballs.

SAUCE FOR MEATBALLS

Brown in butter 1 medium-size can mushroom bits, well drained; 1 pinch marjoram flakes; ⅛ tsp. season salt. Add 2 cups water and stir. To mixture add two tbsp. catsup and one tsp. prepared horseradish mustard and 1 tsp. Worchestershire sauce. Mix to a paste 3 tsp. flour and ¼ cup of the stock from the meatballs. Stir into the simmering mixture enough of the paste to thicken. Keep meatballs hot in sauce. Serve with toothpicks.

Arrange on a platter samples of your favorite deer sausage. These will vary according to your favorite sausage makers. Ours are metwurst, bologna, and summer sausage. The bologna can be served hot or cold. Try slicing the summer sausage very thin, roll a bit of colby cheddar cheese inside, and heat in the oven or over charcoal, skewered with stuffed olives.

Got a gang coming over? Try the hors d'oeuvres with a Colorado casserole and spinach salad.

COLORADO CASSEROLE

1 small boneless venison ham, about 7 lbs. Wrap ham completely in aluminum foil and bake in a roasting pan at 320 degrees, 4½ hours. Remove from oven and cool. (Can be prepared day ahead.) Slice thinly.

3 cans Spanish rice
1 small can crushed pineapple, drained
½ medium onion, diced
1 tbsp. marjoram flakes
1 tsp. season salt

Combine rice, pineapple, onion, and seasonings. Put half of rice mixture in roasting pan. Add ham, then remaining rice mixture. Heat in 270 degree oven 1½ hours. Serves 20.

To complete your buffet fill a large wooden bowl with fresh, crisp spinach. Serve with a sweet-sour hot sauce.

SWEET-SOUR HOT SAUCE

Boil together 1 cup vinegar
1 cup sugar
2 cups water
1 tsp. salt
A little onion flavoring
A pinch celery seed
A dash pepper

(these measures need not be accurate)
Keep hot
Fry out ½ lb. bacon, diced fine
Add to hot liquid, keep hot over a candle holder

Have bowls ready and tongs for spinach, plus a ladle for the sauce. Strictly a help yourself dish (be sure you have enough for seconds . . . it's delicious!).

There is such a great variety of meals that can be conjured up. How about a good old Saskatchewan goulash for a starter?

SASKATCHEWAN GOULASH

6 *lbs. venison, ¾ inch cubes*	*1 pinch caraway seeds*
¼ *lb. butter or margarine*	*Mushrooms if desired*
½ *tsp. seasoned salt*	½ *inch strip of lemon peel*
1 *tsp. marjoram*	*1 tsp. prepared horseradish*
1 *tsp. salt*	*mustard*
¼ *tsp. pepper*	¼ *cup catsup*
1 *tbsp. minced onions*	*Flour to thicken*

In a large hot frying pan, brown butter, add meat. Turn to keep from burning. After all cubes cease to look raw, lower heat, sprinkle with rest of ingredients and 2 table-spoons flour. Stir. Add water gradually to cover meat. Simmer several hours till meat is very tender. If gravy is too thin, stir in enough flour paste to make it desired consistency (thin rather than too thick is better when served with dumplings). Serves 10 to 12.

A wonderful companion dish for the goulash is old-fashioned German potato dumplings.

GERMAN POTATO DUMPLINGS

Have boiled and cold (can be cooked day before) 5 large potatoes. Grate or rice potatoes in large bowl or on a floured board. Spread 1½ cups flour over the potatoes. Sprinkle 1½ teaspoons salt over the flour and break 2 eggs over all. Knead lightly till just mixed. Sprinkle flour on a sheet of waxed paper. Make a roll of the dough and cut roll in about 10 to 20 slices. Cut as many squares of bread cubes as amount of slices. Brown the cubes in butter or margarine. Press one cube in the center of each slice and completely enfold cube with dough. Dip hands in flour and form dumplings. Place aside on floured paper. Have ready a large kettle of boiling water, 1 tablespoon salt added. Ten minutes before mealtime drop dumplings into rapidly boiling water and cover. When water comes to a boil again and dumplings start to rise from bottom, remove lid and boil about 8 minutes longer. Serve immediately. (These dumplings are good next day sliced and fried!) Serves 4 to 6.

Try setting off your meal with a side dish of sweet-sour red cabbage. Our favorite recipe comes from Marg's mother's kitchen, along with the aforementioned dumplings.

SWEET-SOUR RED CABBAGE

Shred 1 large red cabbage and 1 tart red apple. Cover with water and simmer till tender. Drain, then, using the liquid from the cabbage to measure 2 cups (in a separate pan), add:

1 cup white vinegar	*A little pepper*
1 cup sugar (less if you prefer)	*A little onion*
	Pinch of caraway seed
1 tsp. salt	

Boil 5 minutes. Pour over cabbage and simmer about 5 minutes more, covered.

Finely dice ½ pound bacon and fry out. Pour over all and stir. Serves 6.

Serve a nice crisp bread and coffee or your favorite red wine and you have a most delicious meal you will serve again and again.

Saturday night hamburgers is a standard meal at our house. A good iron frying pan is a must. Flatten your patties and lightly sprinkle each with a little salt, pepper, marjoram flakes, and season salt, plus onions if desired. Have ½ teaspoon butter or margarine and ½ teaspoon other shortening hot in the pan. Place patty, seasoned side down, in the hot grease.

While meat is browning have ready bowls of crisp lettuce and favorite dressings. Hard rolls are the best for hamburgers, but any other will do for the bun. Butter and toast the buns and have ready a whipped salad dressing, catsup, mustard, onions, and pickles. Let each build their own! Warning! If kids of college age or lower are present, you better have plenty!

Select your beverages. Top it off with an ice cream sundae. Again allow each to build his own.

Good Old Pennsylvania Rump Roast or Boneless Round

This goes directly from the freezer into a 350-degree oven. Put a little butter in the bottom of the pan, place roast in the pan, sprinkle with season salt, pepper, onion flakes, and marjoram flakes. Roast, uncovered, for about 2 to 2½ hours (depending on size of roast, figuring 20 minutes to the pound and ½ hour extra to thaw). Baste with butter halfway through. If the roast is boneless, turn it once. Remove from the oven and allow to set for 10 minutes before slicing. Arrange slices on a hot platter. Serve with baked potatoes, sour cream with chives, and hot rolls. For vegetable, serve peas and carrots or green beans. As a very tasty garnish, pass a dish of mint jelly.

We must not forget the frying meat. The tenderloins are especially nice fried whole, sliced in half, lengthwise, pounded flat with a little flour, broiled . . . you name it. We always use a little sprinkling of marjoram flakes in the frying process. Heat fat (half butter or margarine is a must for best results, with other shortenings) and fry quickly.

Baked potatoes, or toast and a tangy salad, make great companion dishes. Hot rolls, hot bread, and always red wine complete the feast.

Hats off to the Swiss for my taste favorite.

Swiss Steak

Be sure to trim *all* the fat from the slices of round you will want to use for this dish. Preheat the oven to 325 degrees. Again you will want a large heavy iron frying pan and a small roaster. (An electric fryer can be used if it is a deep one.)

Cut the meat (2 to 2½ pounds) into pieces about 2 inches square. Dip each piece in flour and pound flat on a board. Brown in hot fat and shift to roaster again using half shortening and a spoonful of butter or margarine. When all the meat has been browned and shifted, pour 1 cup water with ½ cup catsup added, into hot fat and simmer for 2 or 3 minutes, until all crisp lifts from the bottom of the pan. Add ½-inch strip of lemon peel, ½ teaspoon marjoram flakes, 1 tablespoon minced onion, ½ teaspoon salt, ¼ teaspoon pepper, and simmer another minute. Pour over meat, adding enough water to just cover. Bake until meat is very tender. Thicken before serving. Serves 4 to 6.

Boiled potatoes and rye bread go well with this dish. Vegetables can be anything you desire. This makes a very hearty meal that can be prepared way ahead, even frozen. Each time it's heated it tastes better!

And now we arrive at the *meat* of this chapter! Some of the more exotic types of meat dishes. A particularly tasty dish is

Braised Venison Shank

For this you should have four shanks of venison. (You will have to remember not to bone these portions when preparing the meat for the freezer.)

2 cups Burgundy wine	1 pinch thyme (optional)
2 cups consommé (beef)	1 cup diced celery
Sprig parsley	1 cup diced onions
1 bay leaf	1 cup diced carrots
2 peppercorns	3 tbsp. butter or margarine
1 pinch marjoram	3 tbsp. flour
1 small clove garlic, cut	

Dredge meat in flour, brown in a little butter. Add 4 cups liquid and herbs. Cover and cook in Dutch oven or braise in oven for 1½ to 2 hours at 350 degrees. Add the 3 cups vegetables and cook till tender, about ½ hour longer. Remove shanks and vegetables. Make a paste of 3 tablespoons flour and butter and add to remaining liquid to make gravy. Return vegetables and shanks, salt and pepper to taste. Serves 4.

Meat Loaf

3 lbs. venisonburger	1 tbsp. catsup
6 slices bread, need not be dry	1 tsp. salt
	¼ tsp. pepper
1 small can condensed milk	½ cup finely diced celery
1 tbsp. minced onion	1 thick slice bacon
2 eggs	Catsup or 1 can (10 oz.)
½ tsp. marjoram	tomato soup

Tear up bread in very small pieces. Mix egg, and milk, and catsup and pour over bread. Add rest of ingredients and mix well. Form a loaf and place in roaster. Pour soup over loaf, or garnish with catsup and slice of bacon. Bake in preheated 350 degree oven about 1½ hours, uncovered. Add a little water as needed, but do not pour over the meat so that you do not wash off soup or disturb garnish. Serves 8.

SWEDISH MEATBALLS

MEATBALLS

¾ cup oats (quick or old fashioned, uncooked)
½ cup milk
1 egg
¼ cup grated onion
1 tsp. salt
¼ tsp. pepper
½ tsp. ground mace

2 tsp. Worcestershire sauce
1 lb. ground venison, juice of ½ lemon added and mixed well with venison before adding any other ingredients
Dash of tabasco

SAUCE

2 tbsp. all-purpose flour
½ tsp. salt
⅛ tsp. pepper

2 cups milk
1 tsp. Worcestershire sauce
Dash of tabasco

For meatballs, combine all ingredients thoroughly. Shape to form small meatballs, using about 1 tablespoon meat mixture for each. Brown in small amount of shortening in large skillet, turning frequently until browned on all sides. Add ¼ cup water. Cover; simmer 30 minutes. Remove from heat.

For sauce, remove meatballs and drain off all but about 2 tablespoons drippings from pan. Add flour, salt, and pepper to drippings in pan; mix well. Add milk and Worcestershire sauce. Simmer about five minutes or until thickened, stirring frequently. Add meatballs. Heat thoroughly. Sprinkle with snipped parsley. Makes 48 meatballs.

VENISON TEXAS STYLE

3 tbsp. olive oil
2 lbs. vension steak, trimmed
     and cut into ½-inch cubes
1 tsp. marjoram
Salt and freshly ground pep-
     per to taste
4 tbsp. butter or margarine
2 large Italian sweet peppers
     thinly sliced

1 large onion chopped
1 clove garlic, finely chopped
10 to 12 medium sized fresh
     mushrooms, thinly sliced
1 can (No. 202) tomatoes
1½ cups fresh or canned
     tomato sauce
1 tbsp. flour

Heat olive oil in a large skillet over moderate heat. Fry venison cubes until browned, adding the marjoram, salt and pepper.

In another skillet heat half the butter and cook the peppers, onion, garlic, and mushrooms. Sauté over low heat for about 8 to 10 minutes, stirring constantly.

Combine the venison, onion, and mushroom mixture, tomatoes, and tomato sauce and simmer 45 minutes, stirring frequently

Combine the flour with remaining butter to make a smooth paste and stir this, bit by bit, into the sauce. Cook ten minutes longer. Serve over cooked egg noodles. Serves 4.

SOUTH DAKOTA STUFFED VENISON STEAK ROLLS

1 venison round steak, cut in
     half lengthwise
2 slices bacon, cut three times
     ordinary thickness
2 slices dill pickle

Flour, salt, pepper
Shortening
½ cup catsup
1 tsp. Worcestershire sauce
½ cup water

Place bacon and pickle on each strip of venison. Roll up and fasten with string. Roll in flour seasoned with salt and pepper. Place in heavy skillet in which shortening has been heated. Brown on all sides. When browned, add catsup, sauce, and water, which have been mixed together. Cover and simmer on top of stove for one hour. Serves 2.

ROLADEN FLEISCH

You will need about eight pieces of flank, about 4 inches square, pounded flat. Sprinkle with salt and pepper. Spread with a thin layer of prepared horseradish mustard. In the center of each piece place several ¼-inch strips of bacon and a light sprinkling of minced onion and several thin slivers of carrots. Roll up and fasten at each end with toothpick, or tie up with store string.

In heavy iron skillet melt 2 tablespoons butter or margarine. Add several pinches of marjoram flakes and a light sprinkle of season salt. Brown roladen and place in a small roaster.

Pour ½ cup water in skillet and simmer until all crisps rise from bottom. Pour over meat in roaster and place in oven preheated to 325 degrees. Bake until very tender, about 1 hour, adding water ½ cup at a time as needed. Serves 4.

MONTANA HUNTER'S PIE

Cut any type of venison into small pieces. Cover with water and boil till tender. Thicken gravy with flour and add cooked vegetable—peas, carrots, tomatoes, celery. Season with salt and pepper, one onion, and one garlic clove, chopped fine. Place in a casserole, cover with hot mashed potatoes and bake in 450 degree oven till potatoes are brown.

Nebraska Stew

3 lbs. lean venison cut into 2- by 2- by 1-inch pieces
6 oz. beef fat cut into small pieces
2 tbsp. salt
1 tsp. seasoned salt
1 pinch black pepper
2 pinches dried marjoram leaves
2 medium onions, quartered
1 large rutabaga, cut into ½-inch cubes
2 lbs. carrots, cut to size you like to eat
6 large stalks celery, cut in small pieces
5 large potatoes cut into boiling chunks
1 small head white cabbage, cut into 6 wedges

Place venison, beef fat, and 6 quarts of water into a minimum 8 quart kettle, and bring to a boil; simmer until the meat is almost as tender as you want it. Skim occasionally, remove most of the fat chunks that are left. Add seasonings, onions, celery, rutabaga, and carrots. Bring almost to a boil, simmer 20 to 25 minutes. If you intend to eat the stew all in one meal, and do not intend to freeze it, add the potatoes at this time. If you intend to freeze it, cook the potatoes separately and add to your plate at the table. In 10 minutes add the cabbage and cook for 15 minutes. Serve with hot fresh bread and soft butter. There won't be any left if six hungry hunters tackle it!

French Canadian Roast Venison with Red Wine and Onions

1 4 lb. venison roast
Salt, pepper
½ tsp. marjoram
1 clove garlic, minced
6 diced yellow onions—small
Butter
1 cup sour red wine

Rub roast with salt, pepper, garlic, and marjoram. Place it in a preheated 400-degree oven and brown on all sides. Reduce heat to 300 degrees. Roast 1 hour and 20 minutes for rare meat. Sauté onions in a large lump of butter until they are a golden color. Add wine and water until onions are covered. Cover kettle and simmer one hour. Remove roast to a hot platter. Stir onion sauce into roasting pan and mix with drippings. Cook and stir until onions become mushy. Skim fat, pour this over roast. Serves 8.

BAVARIAN STYLE POT ROAST

4 to 5 lbs. venison round roast, boneless	2 bay leaves
1 tsp. salt	1 tsp. sugar
¼ tsp. coarsely ground black pepper	1 sliced onion—medium
¼ cup red wine vinegar	1 clove garlic, pressed or minced
1½ cups dry red wine	1 sliced orange
1½ cups water	1 sliced lemon
2 tbsp. brandy	2 tbsp. cooking oil
	3 tbsp. flour

Make a marinade combining all ingredients except cooking oil and flour and cover roast. Refrigerate from 24 to 36 hours, turning frequently. Drain roast and brown in cooking oil. Place meat and marinade in roaster or dutch oven and simmer from 3 to 4 hours or until roast is tender. Remove from pan.

At this point, after the meat has cooled, it can be sliced, reshaped and tied with a string for easier serving. Strain liquid and remove fat. Reserve enough marinade for reheating roast. Thicken the remainder slightly with a flour and water paste. Serve sauce with meat. Serves 12 to 15.

One cup sliced mushrooms and ½ cup dry sherry wine may be added to the strained sauce if you like. Reheat both the sauce and roast in a 350-degree oven for approximately 25 minutes before serving. The flavor of the meat will be improved if it is basted or turned during simmering period. Serve with buttered noodles.

California Spicy Rump Roast

1 venison roast, 5 lb. rump	½ tsp. seasoned salt
1 cup Burgundy wine	⅛ tsp. garlic powder
2 tbsp. wine vinegar	2 or 3 tbsp. drippings or oil
⅓ cup broth or water	⅓ cup chili sauce
½ tsp. dried marjoram	1 tbsp. instant minced onion

Lard the roast by piercing the meat with a long, thin knife or a skewer and pushing strips of chilled larding pork (salt pork) into the incisions, or wrap slices of larding pork around the meat and fasten it with a string.

Combine wine, vinegar, broth, marjoram, salt, and garlic powder. Pour over meat, cover, and marinate in refrigerator overnight, turning several times. Drain well, saving marinade.

Brown meat on all sides in heated drippings or oil. Add chili sauce and onion to drained marinade. Pour half over meat. Cover and cook until tender in hot oven (435 degrees) allowing about 20 minutes for each pound of meat.

Baste with remaining marinade during cooking period. Skim and discard any excess fat from pan juices; thicken remaining liquid if desired. Makes 8 to 10 servings.

Wisconsin Rolled Haunch Roast Spit Style

6 lbs. boneless haunch roast	Dry marjoram leaves, or sprig
½ lb. beef fat cut into long	of fresh marjoram
strips	Salt and pepper
Butter or margarine to baste	½ lemon or ½ orange
with	

Place roast on spit. With a sharp knife cut incisions ¼ to ½ inch deep, 1 inch apart, parallel to spit. Pin beef fat around the roast the opposite way with toothpicks at 1-

inch intervals. The coals should be hot and enough fire must be maintained for 2½ to 3 hours. When outside of roast gets hot, baste with butter in between beef fat. Immediately after basting, sprinkle marjoram leaves on by crushing between fingers (or fasten fresh sprig across center) over the roast. In a half hour or so squeeze lemon or orange juice every half hour until roast is done to your taste. The last half hour sprinkle salt and pepper on roast as it goes around. Rare: 2 to 2½ hours. Medium: 2½ to 3 hours. Prick with fork to see how it juices. Remove from heat and let set 10 minutes. Cut ½-inch-thick slices with a sharp knife. Serves 14 to 18.

Serve on hot plates with a baked potato from the grill, vegetable of your choice, good red wine, and mustard, horseradish or A-1 sauce for the meat if you like.

Minnesota Spitted Loin

1 to 2½ lb. shoulder loins (depending on how many persons to be served) with all sinew carefully removed	*3 to 6 slices of thickly cut bacon, ⅛ inch or better, preferably from good slab bacon* *A smidgin' of garlic salt*

Split loins the long way and cut ¼-inch deep incisions an inch apart parallel to the spit. Pin 3 strips of bacon lengthwise on each loin, using toothpicks to fasten. Cook on hot fire 40 to 60 minutes (depending on size of loin; allow 8 ounces per person). The last 10 minutes sprinkle lightly with garlic salt.

Slice ½-inch thick and serve on a hot plate with whatever your heart desires. The only thing you'll remember about this meal will be the meat and the company.

STUFFED HEART

Soak heart in salted water overnight or all day. Drain for a few minutes, rub inside with a little salt. Stuffing:

2 cups bread cubes	Generous pinch marjoram
1 large stem celery, diced fine . . . include some leaves	flakes
	Enough milk to moisten bread with 1 tbsp. melted
1 tbsp. diced onion	butter added

Cut out center of heart (use good parts, free of membranes, cut up fine and add to dressing) and replace with stuffing. Close up with skewers, or sew with store string as tightly as possible. Place heart in roasting pan suitable for size and pour over it ½ cup water and 3 tablespoons brandy. Bake covered at 350 degrees for 1½ to 2 hours, or until tender. Add more water if necessary and baste occasionally.

Serve with a favorite salad or vegetable. Generally one heart will be enough for two people. If you want to invite more for a taste, try stretching with

PAN-FRIED LIVER

Wash liver in cold water. Skin the liver. Refrigerating or freezing for a few hours before using makes it easier to handle and is better for pan frying.

About an hour before mealtime melt 4 tablespoons butter or margarine in a frying pan. Dip slices of liver into lemon juice. Slice 2 large onions into frying pan and sauté about 10 minutes, until tender but not brown. Set onions aside in a warmed dish and quickly fry liver slices until just done (a little rare, if you can sell the idea). When liver is ready, on a *hot* platter, heap with onion and serve immediately. Must be from skillet to table.

Remove heart from oven and slice onto a heated platter, with some of the juices from the pan poured over it.

These two dishes are a great "after the hunt" feast . . . a real treat for the hunters.

A favorite version of venison is this gourmet concoction made with Burgundy wine. This particular dish looks expensive and complicated, but in reality makes life easy for the cook!

FRENCH STEW

4 tbsp. butter or margarine
3 lbs. boneless venison rump cut into 1½-inch cubes
¼ cup brandy
2 beef bouillon cubes dissolved in 1 cup boiling water
1½ cups red Burgundy wine
1 tsp. salt
¼ tsp. pepper
½ tsp. marjoram flakes
2 tbsp. frozen chopped parsley
2 strips bacon, diced
1 bag (1 lb. 4 oz.) frozen small whole onions
1 pkg. (6 oz.) frozen whole mushrooms

In a large skillet melt the butter and brown the beef well on all sides.

In a small saucepan heat brandy until warm. With a match, light the brandy and pour flaming over venison. Shake skillet until flames die.

Transfer venison and pan juices to casserole that has bouillon, wine, salt, pepper, marjoram, and parsley. Cover tightly with foil, then cover with lid and cook in a preheated oven at 350 degrees until meat is tender . . . usually about 2 hours.

About 10 minutes before meat is done, cook bacon in

skillet, add frozen onions and mushrooms, cover, and cook over medium heat until vegetables are thawed and tender, about 5 minutes. Uncover and continue cooking until liquid has evaporated and vegetables are lightly browned. Add to beef mixture. If you like, sprinkle with additional parsley. Serves 6 to 8 people.

Something different, delicious and easy to prepare, really convenient for the working mother, is this Mississippi Casserole, which is great for ovens that can be preset and timed automatically.

Mississippi Casserole

1 lb. venison, cut in 2 inch cubes

½ cup Burgundy, claret, or other red dinner wine

1 (10½ oz.) can undiluted condensed consommé

¾ tsp. salt

⅛ tsp. pepper

1 medium-size onion, sliced (1 tbsp. dried onion flakes can be substituted)

¼ cup fine dry bread crumbs

¼ cup sifted all-purpose flour

Combine raw meat, wine, consommé, salt, pepper, and onion in casserole. Mix flour with crumbs; stir into casserole mixture and cover. Preset your oven at slow (300 degree) to allow about 3 hours of cooking time. Serve with buttered carrots and rice. Serves 4.

Here are several different stews, all of them delicious and mouth-watering. Who can resist the wonderful aroma of stew cooking in the kitchen?

GOLD RUSH STEW

4 lbs. lean venison	*3 tbsp. chopped parsley*
⅓ cup flour	*2 bay leaves*
4 tbsp. olive oil	*2 sprigs marjoram*
Salt and freshly ground black pepper	*1 small piece orange peel*
½ lb. bacon, diced	*1 bottle red wine*
2 cloves garlic	*Beurre manie*
2 carrots, diced	*12 ripe olives, pitted*
2 cups small white onions	*12 mushrooms, sliced*

Cut meat into large cubes, roll them in flour, and brown on all sides in melted butter and olive oil. Transfer to a casserole, and season to your taste with salt and freshly ground black pepper.

Sauté diced bacon, garlic, carrots, and onions in remaining fat until bacon is crisp and vegetables are golden brown. Transfer to casserole with meat; add parsley, bay leaves, marjoram, and orange peel. Gradually moisten with one bottle of good red wine and cook in a slow oven (200 degrees) for 1½ hours, or until meat is tender. Stir in, a little at a time, a beurre manie made with 1 tablespoon flour blended to a paste with the same amount of butter. Add pitted ripe olives and sliced mushrooms; cover and allow to simmer in a slow oven until mushrooms are cooked. If desired, add two quartered tomatoes the last few minutes. Serves 8 to 10.

HUNTER'S STEW FROM POLAND

2 tbsp. butter	2 apples, peeled and diced
1 large onion, chopped	½ cup pitted prunes,
1 can beef broth	quartered
2 small pieces of venison	1 tsp. salt
Bologna, about ¼ lb.	Freshly ground pepper to
1 small head cabbage,	taste
shredded	½ cup red wine
1 cup sliced mushrooms	¼ cup water
3 cups sauerkraut	1 clove garlic, pressed
1 can tomato sauce	

Melt butter in stewpot and sauté onion until lightly browned. Add broth, sausage, cabbage, mushrooms, sauerkraut, tomato sauce, apples, prunes, salt, and pepper. Cover and simmer very slowly 1½ hours. Add wine, water, and garlic, and simmer another 40 minutes. If any is left over, it should be stored in the refrigerator in a glass bowl.

Two sauces to try with venison are:

SPANISH SAUCE

2 lbs. venison bones	2 cloves garlic, cut in half,
1 medium onion	optional
2 carrots	2 tbsp. tomato paste
2 stalks celery	1 cup flour (about)
6 whole allspice	2¼ to 3 quarts brown or white
8 to 10 crushed peppercorns	stock (not fish)

Brown venison bones in a large cooking pot. (If they form more than one layer, do not try to brown all bones at the same time.) Cube vegetables and add along with allspice, peppercorns, and garlic; brown vegetables. Add tomato paste and cook, stirring frequently over high heat for three to four minutes. Sprinkle flour over bones and vegetables; stir with a wooden spoon until flour is brown and worked in. Add stock and simmer at least 4 to 5 hours. Strain sauce. (This will make enough sauce for one meal plus leftover sauce to store and use another time.) After straining, add 4 tablespoons dairy sour cream, 1 tablespoon lemon juice, and 3 tablespoons dry white wine.

CUMBERLAND SAUCE

1 tsp. dry English mustard
2 tsp. water
1 cup currant jelly
2 tbsp. cooking sherry
1 tbsp. orange juice
Pinch of cayenne pepper

2 shallots, chopped and blanched
Peel from 1 orange (no white), cut into julienne strips

Mix mustard with water. Put jelly through a fine strainer. Add mustard mixture and all other ingredients.

CANNED VENISON

For the cook who enjoys canning, canned venison has flavor that can't be reproduced in any other way. And it's such a simple process that the most inexperienced cook can try it and wind up with an end product that will bring praise from anyone who tries it. One quart serves 4.

Trim all the fat and bone from the meat and cut it in bite-size cubes. Have ready clean quart jars, lids, and rings.

Pack jars loosely with raw meat cubes; add ⅓ cup cold water, 1 teaspoon salt, and sprinkle a little garlic powder into each jar.

Put lids on jars and wind on rings firmly. Cook in pressure cooker for 1½ hours (or follow the directions for your cooker).

If you prefer to can by the hot-water bath method, place the jars in boiling water (water should cover lids ½ inch) for 4 hours.

There is nothing so handy as a jar of meat canned this way. You will be able to short cut your stews, goulashes, casseroles. Simply open a jar and proceed with your favorite recipe. You can cut it up into salads, too. It all depends on your inventiveness.

FRIED HEARTS AND EGGS FOR THE HUNTERS' CAMP

Slice heart about ¼ inch thick after removing gristle and membrane. Pan fry in smoking-hot shortening, oil, or bacon grease till done. Don't forget to spike the cooking fat with a light sprinkling of seasoned salt.

Heart and eggs are delicious served together with scads of hot buttered toast and steaming coffee (my son-in-law likes hot chocolate with his).

Great for a hunter's breakfast!

BARBECUED VENISON RIBS

If you like lamb ribs barbecued, you will like venison ribs.

You will need about 4 or 5 pounds of ribs, cut into serving pieces. Place ribs in a flat roasting pan, dot with 3 tablespoons of butter, or lay about 4 or 5 strips of thick cut bacon over the piece of ribs. Sprinkle with ½ teaspoon of crushed marjoram leaves. Bake in 325 degree oven for about 1½ hours, or till meat is tender but not dry. Serves 4.

For the barbecue sauce:

¼ *cup salad oil*
2 *medium onions, chopped*
1 *cup catsup*
½ *cup cider vinegar*

½ *cup prepared mustard*
1 *tsp. salt*
1 *tsp. chili powder*
¼ *tsp. black pepper*

(If using blackstrap molasses, add 1 tablespoon brown sugar.)

Fry onions lightly in fat, then add remaining ingredients. Simmer for 5 minutes. Pour excess fat off ribs. Pour barbecue sauce over them, bake for another 30 minutes.

For deer camp, hang ribs by the open fire, or set over coals on a grill. Bring barbecue sauce from home already made. Do not cook meat too fast. Spread barbecue sauce on ribs often and turn ribs often. When they're done, tackle 'em with your fingers!

VENISON, POUNDED AND FRIED

Have meat cut in serving pieces, about ½ inch thick. Pound with dull side of butcher knife or a meat hammer. Have grease smoking hot in skillet.

Mix a little pepper, marjoram flakes, and seasoned salt in a little flour. (For camping I keep a small shortening can with plastic lid filled with flour, already seasoned, in my camp kit.) Dip meat in flour lightly on both sides and place in hot fat. Fry meat to desired doneness. For those who like onions—I keep a tin of dried onion flakes in the camp kit also. Rejuvenate the flakes in a little water and fry them as you would fresh onions and serve on top of meat.

There are some very definite rules to follow when preparing and serving venison. Always serve it piping hot onto heated plates. Venison fat, like lamb fat, has a tendency to set quickly and becomes tallowy when cool. It is also important to keep the remaining servings hot for second helpings, for the same reasons.

I have emphasized trimming as much of the fat as possible before cooking, but it is impossible to remove it all. So, remember: keep venison *hot* for both visual and taste appeal.

Venison has a tendency to be a little dry. Like most all game, there is very little fat interspersed in the muscle tissue. You can avoid this dryness somewhat by adding butter or margarine, and when roasting or frying, do not overcook. Serve rare whenever it's possible. If your guests prefer meat well done, you have no choice; but you can offset the dryness by stopping the heat just as soon as the meat stops juicing, and being ready to serve immediately. (Of course everyone has to co-operate . . . no late comers!) Always spoon some of the juices or gravy over the meat on the *hot* platter; it will look and taste better.

You will notice that in most of the recipes, either wine, vinegar, or lemon is included. These do not interfere with the natural good flavor of venison; they simply enhance the taste and help to retain the natural juices and aid in tenderizing the meat.

Sköl!

II. Tidbits

Winter, with its snow and ice, used to be a season of tranquil beauty which all pursued things used as a quiet to recoup themselves from the strenuous, young-rearing times of summer and the hunting invasions in the fall. Winter gave the animals time to forget about man and his noxious (to animals) ways. This is the period when the animals, particularly deer, need a respite from the constant pressures of man. Deer are not equipped with the rationalizing brains of humans. Either a deer fears today or it does not fear. If deer could actually think of things present and gone by, I'm sure they would think that years ago humans hibernated in the winter, because they just didn't see them. The only motors a deer heard were snowplows and an occasional car braving the winter roads.

197

Now, after the first fall of snow, an area is turned into a whitened super highway for snarling snowmobiles to take people where people don't belong. The snow, which slows down or immobilizes other creatures, exhilarates and frees the snowmobilers.

The deer, who treats man on foot as one of life's evils to be lived with but avoided, is suddenly confronted with mobile man who can travel at least twice as fast as any deer can, on a brightly colored machine that, as a noise pollutant, has no equal for its size. This snowmobile's roaring, pounding, reverberating noise can be heard easily for a mile or more in the crisp, still winter air. Is it any wonder that a deer becomes terror-stricken when set upon by a new predator it never knew before?

How can a wild animal possibly interpret your intent? To a deer, any man who proposed "togetherness" between man and deer is bad medicine. Even if you could call out and have them understand you only want to look, I'm not sure they could stand their ground and let you roar past. I even get scared when a snowmobile roars past me 15 feet away, and I'm *almost* sure they're not out to run me down!

Last year at Friess Lake, Wisconsin, a buck and a doe met a very untimely death by drowning shortly after the first snowfall. Two unthinking snowmobilers, after jumping the deer in a fenceline, decided to chase them a "little." The frantic animals panicked and ran out on the thin, snow-covered lake ice. A third of the way across they broke through and, not being able to get out of the hole, drowned. A great tragedy? Perhaps not, if you are a human.

Imagine, if you can, a reverse situation. You know all about snapping turtles and how vicious they can be. One bite and a chunk out of your leg or finger is gone. These things are dangerous, but easily avoided, because any human being, including small children, can outrun or dodge one easily, and in the fall they are gone until the spring; no worries in the winter. (I am speaking of the snow states.) Now, all of a sudden the snappers are given a mobility you never dreamed of. They rise out of the mud at the first snow, and begin cruising the cities and towns, skimming along easily at twice the speed of any man, woman, or child. The snapper has also developed the ability to growl like a mad lion, popping his jaws at the same time! I don't know about you, friend, but even if they didn't intend to bite, they would scare me and the kids! I also know this, humans would get rid of this menace immediately, even if they had to call out the Army, Navy, and Marines!

Game wardens are finding deer these winters in areas that they have not frequented other winters. They tell me that snowmobiles are the reason. Driven from their usual haunts, deer find other areas, some very marginal, in which to stay.

Now these actions for the most part are not by those irresponsible few, who may try to chase a deer to death if they see one, but these are the actions, in the main, of responsible operators. These are the people who love the snow, the outdoors, *and* the deer. These people only want to see the deer in the winter, not kill it. They only want to show other people the deer, but in order to love something truly you must have an understanding of it. These same well-meaning souls wouldn't hesitate to turn in a game violator if they saw one, or would scream to high heaven if they saw deer being harassed by dogs.

A friend of mine bought a snowmobile mainly to give

his small children a ride. I knew of a picked cornfield that the deer were using for their prime feeding ground. This field was the only one in a fairly large deer area. I watched the deer for a couple of weeks from the road with my spotting scope, and had counted 21 deer feeding there at one time. There was an excellent bed ground less than a 100 yards from the field, consisting of thick conifers with a southern exposure. The deer were in an ideal situation. Then I noticed suddenly that there were fewer deer in the field every evening. In a matter of three days there were none! My first thought was that they had cleaned up the field, but I quickly dismissed this as I knew they hadn't even covered a twentieth of the field; then I thought that perhaps dogs had chased them out.

While I was pondering this and making up my mind to snowshoe back there and see what was going on, I ran into this friend of mine. He immediately began to tell me how many deer he had been seeing now that he had a snowmobile. My ears perked up and I asked him if he would take me on one of those little rides. Sure thing, but I would have to dress warm, because it's been below zero every night now. Also we might not see deer, 'cause he hadn't seen any for a couple nights, but we would try it anyway. I dressed warm and we set out just after sundown. We zipped across the road and onto a well-packed snowmobile trail. One mile, or not more than two minutes, later we were right at the bed ground, then seconds later we were crossing the cornfield.

"No deer here tonight again," said John, "I wonder where they went. Maybe we're too early. I generally come out a little later."

That explained why I hadn't heard or seen the snowmobile while I was observing the deer from a half mile away.

I jumped on him with both feet.

"You're the one who chased them away, you dimwit! Didn't it ever occur to you that you were disrupting hell out of those deer? You've not disrupted their habits, but you caused them to go on a completely different feed, which they are not used to, and at 20 degrees below zero!" I harangued.

"I only wanted to look at them and show my kids," he said defensively, "they have never seen deer that close before."

"With guys like you around, your kids may never see them that close again," I countered.

"They'll be back, I won't bother them again," John said, a little shamefaced.

Those deer never did return to that spot all winter. Who knows how many didn't make it because of the change. This guy was not a bad guy intentionally, only unknowingly.

Game wardens and biologists tell me that one single extra effort required by a deer to avoid harassment could mean the difference between life or death in the dead of winter.

There are authenticated cases in Wisconsin, Minnesota, and Michigan, of deer dying of pneumonia after being chased by snowmobiles. It's hard to understand how such a tough, adaptable animal can be so fragile at times, yet there are many cases of man himself, perishing from exposure to the elements for a single night. The great white wolf called winter gets more vicious than ever in the latter part of the season. The deer that could survive a molestation in January will perish from the same in the latter part of February. By late winter the snow-country whitetail is in a weakened condition, even if things are favorable.

The snowmobile makes a path and packs the snow. This could be helpful on northern areas of deep snow, inasmuch as deer have been seen using these tracks quite frequently. It's a lot better than plowing through all that snow. But again, what's good for the deer is also good for the coyote, or even two-legged predators who wouldn't ordinarily get in the deep-snow country. This also provides another hazard. Deer using snowmobile paths are inclined to run on these paths when they hear a snow-mobile coming. When the snowmobile gets too close, the deer are forced to leave the path and struggle to get away through as much as 4 feet of snow. This effort could be the breaking point, and if it occurs several times, the end result is death in an agonizing way. Perhaps if a series of trails were broken once for the deer, then completely abandoned by machines, there could be a definite benefit. I'm sure there are a lot of sportsmen who will, in time of need, grab their chainsaws, jump on their trusty snowmobiles and get back in to cut browse for deer who would starve without help. Bless these guys!

What can be done to promote a harmonious condition between snowmobiles and deer? In order to preserve nature's immutable laws, snow states must legislate promptly to (1) limit snowmobile use to specifically marked trails or designated "open" areas where they will be unable to harass any animal in any manner, especially "yarded" deer; (2) absolutely forbid the use of snowmobiles for hunting or trapping purposes, chasing game, or joy riding in hunting areas during the game seasons.

I don't think any of us are ready to accept the continued eroding of man's or animal's basic right to peace and quiet. The deer might say, "Forgive them for they know not what they do."

I say, "Educate them, so they know what they're doing!"

Knife selection is not difficult. A good knife should not be too large. A blade of 3½ to 4½ inches is just right. The main requirement of a good knife is that it be the best steel so it will hold an edge well. There is some controversy about the shape of the knife. I prefer a folding knife to a straight one, but this is purely a matter of choice. A pocket or folding knife that doesn't have a lock to hold the blade open can devastate your fingers. If you keep your knife as sharp as possible, deer dressing and camp chores will be a lot easier. Don't forget to take a pocket hone along to camp so you can touch up the blade occasionally.

Carry a compass with you just in case of heavy fog, heavy snow, or darkness, but don't try to use it near any metal, including your belt buckle. It won't lie to you, believe it!

Don't lace your boots too tight.

Make sure you have extra gloves or mitts along.

Several layers of light clothing are warmer than one heavy one.

Carry your knife, watch, light nylon ropes, paraffin fire starters, waterproof matches, toilet paper, chap stick, snack, camera (if you can), plastic bag, and police whistle for signaling.

Here's how to make the snack: mix equal portions of

raisins, cashew nuts, good peanuts, and sweet chocolate bits. Put 4 ounces, or more if you like, of the mixture into heavy plastic bag, and take a package along every day. In an emergency this will keep you going all night.

If you get turned around in the woods, don't panic! Stay where you are, build a fire, eat your snack, and wait.

Carry your ammo where you can get at it, but don't let it jingle.

At camp have aspirin, cold medication, mentholatum, cough drops, hand lotion, stomach alkalizer, brandy, any special medicine you require, plastic bags, deodorant soap, cards, extra car key, spare rifle or shotgun, foot powder.

Hide some object somewhere in the carcass of your deer so you can positively identify it in case it is stolen.

Take a boy hunting.

Hunt trophy-size bucks only for one year.

Don't holler at the cook.

Send a card to your wife.

Keep clean, but no need to shave!

The Wisconsin deer hunter has almost one chance in five to kill a deer, any deer, but on the average only one hunter in nine will get a buck. Theoretically, this means a party of eight, hunting the full nine days of the season, would not tag a single buck. Or, if you and your partner both got bucks, a party of sixteen could conceivably not hang a single buck on the pole!

Know how to play cards well!

If you forgot the alarm, use the Indian method. Drink an extra glass of water or an extra cup of coffee before you go to bed.

If at all possible, carry binoculars with you all the time;

they are worth their weight in brandy. It is a lot easier to look for game with a 7×35 wide-angle binocular than with your rifle scope. There is a lot less arm movement with binoculars than with the scope, and the field of view is ten times as much.

Get maps for the areas you intend to hunt, and learn how to read and use them. Maps are generally available in many places, wherever you live. Information concerning maps of your area may be obtained by writing the Map Information Office, Geological Survey, Washington, D.C. 20025.

For instance, you can get a topographical index from them for your state, so you know which map or maps to buy. Get their topographic map symbol sheet; it gives you all you have to know about topo maps.

The 7.5 minute map shows you the greatest detail. The shape of the land portrayed by contours is the distinctive characteristic of topo maps. Contours are imaginary lines following the ground surface at a constant elevation above sea level. The contour interval is the regular elevation difference separating adjacent contour lines on maps. Contour intervals depend on ground slope and map scale; they vary from 5 to 200 feet. Small contour intervals are used for flat terrain; larger intervals for rugged mountain areas. Supplementary dashed or dotted contours, at less than the regular interval, are used in flat areas. Index contours, every fourth or fifth line, are heavier than others and have elevation figures. Hachures, form lines, and symbol patterns are also used to show some kinds of topographic forms. Relief shading, an overprint giving a three-dimensional effect, is used on some quadrangle maps.

Colors distinguish classes of map features. Black is

used for manmade or cultural features, such as roads, buildings, names, and boundaries. Blue is used for water or hydrographic features, such as lakes, rivers, canals, and glaciers. Brown is used for relief or hydrographic features—land shapes portrayed by contours or hachures. Green is used for woodland cover, with typical patterns to show scrub, vineyards, or orchards. Red emphasizes important roads, shows built-up urban areas, and public-land subdivision lines.

States index circulars show maps published. For each state, and for Puerto Rico and the Virgin Islands, index circulars show all maps distributed. Index maps give quadrangle location and name, survey date, and publisher (if other than the Geological Survey). Listed also are special maps and sheets with prices, map agents and Federal distribution centers, map reference libraries, and detailed instructions for ordering topographic maps.

By procuring and studying topographical maps, you can become fairly familiar with strange territory before you ever set a foot in the area. You will even discover things about familiar territory that you never knew were there. I remember looking at a topo map of a territory that I thought I knew intimately. In the middle of a very wet, thick, swampy area was a tiny area of not more than an acre that was denoted by a tiny brown contour line being around it. The swamp was considered unhuntable because of the water and heavy brush. I never knew that island was there, so I decided to investigate. I put on hip boots, took a bearing, and made my way very slowly to the island. It was there, all right, just like the map said, and it rose probably 4 feet above the marsh. The island was covered with heavy grass and a few popple. When I came up on the island, a great old whitetail buck stood up and looked at me stupidly, as though he had expected anything but a human being to be on his island! He waited entranced until I decked him with a perfect neck shot. This island was an ideal hideout, and from the looks of it I suspect this old boy had spent more than one hunting season riding out the storm there. I admit it was a terrific job dragging that buck out of there, but it was worth it for such a trophy. I didn't dress him out until I got back to the "mainland" because of all the water.

Carry 10 to 12 feet of ¼-inch nylon or ⅜-inch regular rope so you'll have a means of dragging out your deer.

Do take photos, at least back at camp, so you have something to look at later.

If you really want a trophy buck or an outsized bragging specimen, study the North American record book for where they are.

Canada holds forty-one places of the first hundred in the book, so this is a lighted indicator. Saskatchewan is the leader, with twenty-seven places. In fact, Saskatchewan holds 28 percent of all the qualifiers in the record book. Now, before you dash to the province to collect your record-book giant, be advised that an alien may not pursue the wily whitetail in all of Saskatchewan, but is limited to the southeast corner. This will hold you back a somewhat, but Manitoba is a swell place, too.

In the States, trophies are where you find them, with Arkansas leading with nine (of the first hundred), Minnesota a close second with eight, North Dakota next with six, Texas with five, then Montana, New York, Ohio, and Nebraska with four each. The rest are scattered all over the country.

This indicates several things: one, more than half of all the recorded trophies come from an area roughly 900 miles long by 350 miles wide in North Central United States and South Central Canada; two, outside of Minnesota these are lightly hunted areas, which means the deer have a chance to "age." Also the hunter is more adept at hunting and knowledgeable of where the big ones are. In all cases the states with the most hunters and the largest kills fare the poorest in the record category. The states that limit whitetail hunting for periods, then open the season to residents (who have had their eyes open) kill some real busters.

I am sure there are a great many heads that would qualify for the records but the owners never considered entering them. The facts remain, however, that trophies need time to become trophies, and in heavily hunted areas those deer that have managed to become trophies die a natural death because they are wise to man, or are bumped off by automobiles because they don't understand them.

One other interesting feature is that hardly ever is more than one trophy registered from one town, although Saskatchewan did have three repeaters in the first hundred places. This would indicate to me that a record buck whitetail is an oddity of some sort, ranking with men over 7 feet tall, elephants with 100-pound ivory, etc. There are a lot of "good, big heads," but not very many qualified for the book. It takes a truly big rack of horns in order to qualify. Most of those "big" ten-pointers will score in the 130 to 145 points category, but 170 is the minimum, so a qualifier would need half another antler to make it!